INNovation:
Creativity Techniques
for Hospitality Managers

INNovation:
Creativity Techniques
for Hospitality Managers

by

Florence Berger
School of Hotel Administration
Cornell University

and

Dennis H. Ferguson
School of Hotel Administration
Cornell University

John Wiley & Sons, Inc.
New York   Chichester   Brisbane   Toronto   Singapore

Recognizing the importance of preserving what has been written, it is a policy of John Wiley & Sons, Inc. to have books of enduring value published in the United States printed on acid-free paper, and we exert our best efforts to that end.

Copyright ©1990 by John Wiley & Sons, Inc.

All rights reserved. Published simultaneously in Canada.

Reproduction or translation of any part of this work beyond that permitted by Section 107 or 108 of the 1976 United States Copyright Act without the permission of the copyright owner is unlawful. Requests for permission or further information should be addressed to the Permissions Department, John Wiley & Sons, Inc.

This publication is designed to provide accurate and authoritative information in regard to the subject matter covered. It is sold with the understanding that the publisher is not engaged in rendering legal or other professional service. If legal advice or other expert assistance is required, the services of a competent professional person should be sought. From a Declaration of Principles jointly adopted by a Committee of the American Bar Association and a Committee of Publishers.

Library of Congress Cataloging in Publication Data

Berger, Florence, 1943-
    Innovation: creativity techniques for hospitality managers/ Florence Berger, Dennis H. Ferguson.
      p.   cm.
    Includes bibliographical references.
    ISBN 0-471-52774-2
    1. Hospitality industry—Management.   I. Ferguson, Dennis H. II. Title.   III. Title: Innovation.
TX911.3.M27B47   1990
647.94'068—dc20
                                                      90-12328
                                                         CIP

Printed in the United States of America

90 91 10 9 8 7 6 5 4 3 2 1

To our mothers, Belle and Garnet,
who created us with unconditional love.

PREFACE

In the early days of the modern hospitality industry, Ellsworth M. Statler preached that success depended on three things: location, location, location. During this same era Henry Ford was saying, "You can get a Model T in any color as long as it's black."

Today Fords come in colors with names like "light crystal blue," "titanium," and "sandalwood frost."

Similarly, competition and change have forced hospitality organizations to develop qualities that go beyond a good location. We have reached an age in which success depends upon the ability to stand out and to excel. Hospitality managers must constantly look for new ways to offer new and better products. Customers have expressed an increasing demand for hospitality experiences that are "unique" or "different from all the rest." We have reached an age in which success depends upon innovation, innovation, innovation.

Every innovation begins with a creative idea. Thus, the hospitality organization that can learn to generate the best creative ideas is the one that is destined for success. But can people learn to be more creative? Yes. Creativity is not a mystical gift bestowed upon a lucky few. Rather, it is a way of thinking and approaching problems which can be learned.

This book will teach you how to generate creative ideas. The techniques that you will learn in this book will lead you to ideas that can result in innovations. We hope that they will also help you think and live more creatively.

Becoming more creative can lead to personal and financial growth for you and your organization, and, if your innovation changes the hospitality industry, it might just make the whole world a better place to stay.

ACKNOWLEDGMENTS

We are indebted to the following people for their contributions:

- Larry Berger, whose brilliant wit and writing expertise made him a crucial resource for this book.
- Elizabeth Berger Mandell and Jim Mandell, two more exceptionally creative individuals.
- Mike Sullivan, who typed at least 12 drafts of the manuscript, tracked down our peripatetic creative leaders, and cheered us with his excitement on a daily basis.
- Ned Groves, who spent many library hours researching the psychology of selling ideas.
- Claire Thompson, our editor, who saw our vision immediately and supported our efforts enthusiastically. Her keen interest and insight were gratifying.
- Frank Grazioli, our thoughtful and diligent managing editor, who managed the timing of production masterfully.

CONTRIBUTORS

Our deepest gratitude goes to the creative leaders of the hospitality industry, whose wise words provide the core of our book. For their interest in our research and their thoughtful insight, we will always be thankful.

Robert Agnello
President
Koala Inn

John Alexander
President
The CBORD Group Inc.

Anthony Athanas
Restaurateur
Founder and Owner
Anthony's Pier Four
Boston, MA

Richard W. Barger
Chairman
Barger Hotel Corp.
Boston, MA

Joseph H. Baum
President
Joseph Baum & M. Whiteman Co.

Donald Berens
Owner
D. P. Berens, Inc.
Specialty Services
Pittsford, NY

Richard Bradley
Chairman
Bradley Holdings, Ltd.

Hans B. Bremstrom
President
Sara Hotels Management Corp.

Stan Bromley
Regional Vice President/
General Manager
Four Seasons Hotel
Washington

Robert Burns
Chairman
Regent International Hotels

William J. Callnin
President
Atlantic Inns Management,
Inc.

Michael W. N. Chiu
President
Prima Hotels/Holiday Inn
Union City, CA

Robert P. Colombo
General Manager
Grand Hyatt Hotel
New York

Roger Dow
Vice President, Sales &
Marketing Services
Marriott Hotels and Resorts

William V. Eaton
Senior Principal
Cini-Little International

William Eberhardt
Restaurateur
President, Dining Associates

Fred J. Eydt
President
The Watermark Group, Inc.

Charles F. Feeney
Gerard Atkins & Co. Ltd.
London, England

Richard J. Ferris
Former President
United Airlines

Thomas M. Gneiting
Manager—Corporate Services
Federal Express Corp.

Joyce Goldstein
Owner and Chef
Square One Restaurant
San Francisco

Bjorn R. L. Hanson
Managing Director
Laventhol and Horwath

Christopher Hemmeter
Senior Partner
Hemmeter Investment Co.

G. Michael Hostage
Owner
G. M. Hostage, Inc.

Ichiro Inumaru
President/General Manager
Imperial Hotels, Ltd.
Tokyo, Japan

Michael Z. Kay
President
Portman Hotels

J. William Keithan
Formerly Senior Vice President
Westin Hotels and Resorts

J. Peter Kline
President
Harvey Hotels

Michael A. Leven
President
Days Inns

Henri Lewin
Chairman and CEO
Aristocrat Hotels, Inc.

John Mariani
Chairman
Banfi Vintners

J. Willard Marriott, Jr.
President
Marriott Corporation

H. Etienne Merle
Chef/Owner
L'Auberge du Cochon Rouge
Ithaca, NY

Charles J. Mund
President
Service Dynamics Corp.

James E. Petzing
President
CPS Hospitality Management
  Ltd.
James E. Petzing & Associates
  Inc.

James Rouse
The Enterprise Foundation

Stephen Rushmore
President
Hospitality Valuation Services

Burton M. Sack
President and CEO
Pub Ventures of New England, Inc.

Linda Schwabe
Creative Gourmets

John L. Sharpe
Executive Vice President
Four Seasons Hotels, Ltd.

Jim Simonson
Vice President
Restaurants Unlimited, Inc.

H. Jay Sloofman
President
Marketing Visions, Inc.

Leslie W. Stern
President
L. W. Stern Associates, Inc.

Curt R. Strand
Consultant, formerly CEO and Director
Hilton Hotels International

Donald W. Strang
President
Strang Corporation

Keith Talbert
Founder/President
Urban West

Chiaki Tanuma
　Executive Vice President
　Green House Co., Ltd.

Andre S. Tatibouet
　President
　Aston Hotels & Resorts

Jane B. Tatibouet
　Vice President, Human
　　Resources
　Aston Hotels & Resorts

Jonathan Tisch
　President
　Loews Hotels

Donald R. Trice
　President
　Interstate Hotels Corp.

Alice Waters
　Chef/Owner
　Chez Panisse

Hans Weishaupt
　Managing Director
　Statler Hotel and J. W.
　　Marriott Conference Center
　Cornell University

Trisha Wilson
　President
　Wilson & Associates

Carl H. Winston
　Vice President, Operations
　Motels of America

Peter C. Yesawich
  President
  Robinson, Yesawich, and
    Pepperdine

Shoji Yonehama
  President
  Ringer Hut U.S.A.
    Corporation

John Young
  Senior Vice President, Human
    Resources
  Four Seasons Hotels

Contents

Preface vii
Acknowledgments ix
Contributors xi

CHAPTER 1 Introduction 1

Why Be Creative in the Hospitality Industry? 1
What is Creativity and How Can I Get More of It? 4
    Coming Up with Ideas 5
A Working Definition of Creativity 7
The Four Tools of Creativity: Keys, Glue, Remindings, and
    Questions 9
        Keys and Glue
        Remindings
        Questions: The Master Tool

CHAPTER 2 Just You and Your Yellow Pad 13

Technique 1 Free Association 15
Technique 2 Metaphors 17
    Changing the Way It Is
Technique 3 Attribute Listing 22
Technique 4 SCAMPER 24
Technique 5 Matrix Analysis 28
Technique 6 Design Tree 28

CHAPTER 3	Use A Locksmith	33
Technique 7	Lists	35
Technique 8	Tried and True Locksmiths: Proverbs	36
Technique 9	Innovative Imitation	39
Technique 10	Learn About Something Else	40
Technique 11	Let Employees and Staff Know That You and Your Organization Are Eager For Change	41
CHAPTER 4	How Could the Question Be Changed?	45
Technique 12	Question Breakdown	46
Technique 13	Ask Broader and Narrower Questions	47
Technique 14	Ask the Question of a Metaphor	48
Technique 15	Ask Opposite Questions and Inside-Out Questions	49
Technique 16	Ask Precedence and Consequence Questions	50
Technique 17	Ask the "Real" Question	50
Technique 18	Ask This List of Questions	52
	Object Rules	52
	Action Rules	53
Technique 19	Ask Ridiculous Questions	54
Conclusion		55
CHAPTER 5	The Creative Group—How to Make More Heads Better Than One	57
The Speech		59
Discussion Formats		60
Discussion Format 1	Group Brainstorming	
Discussion Format 2	The Nominal Group Technique (NGT)	
Discussion Format 3	A Combination: NGT-Storming	
Discussion Format 4	Question Questing	
CHAPTER 6	How to Choose the Right Ideas	69
The Easy Cases		69

The Situation Gets Tougher	70
Necessary Selection Criteria	
Desirable Selection Criteria	
The Rating Scheme	

CHAPTER 7   Blocks to Creativity and How to Smash Them   75

Six Blocks and Six Sledgehammers	78

CHAPTER 8   Selling Your Ideas   91

Really Know Your Idea	92
Determine Your Buyer and Your Buyer's Needs	93
Know Your Buyer's Communication Style	94
Watch Your Timing	95
Establish a Relationship of Trust	95
Be Creative	96
Making the Presentation	97
The Words You Speak	
The Words You Write	
The Words Your Body Speaks	
The Words You Hear	
Be Patient and Persistent	99

CHAPTER 9   After Words   101

Creative Industry Leaders Focus on Issues Important to the Creative Process	101
Creativity as a Full-time Business	
Rewarding Creativity	
Characteristics That Creative Industry Leaders Emphasize	104
Self-confidence	
Patience to Enable Incubation	
High Energy	
Desire to Learn	
Desired Characteristics of Employees	106
Conclusion	108
Index	109

*INNovation:
Creativity Techniques
for Hospitality Managers*

CHAPTER 1

Introduction

WHY BE CREATIVE IN THE HOSPITALITY INDUSTRY?

This question could be answered with some fancy statistics that demonstrate the link between creativity and financial success, but we would rather let creative leaders in the industry answer the question in their own words. Their answers suggest that creativity leads not only to financial success but to a sense of personal fulfillment. Creativity makes work more fun.

> Without creativity, we have no business. Our company is entirely dependent upon our creativity.
>
> *Chris Hemmeter*
> *Senior Partner*
> *Hemmeter Investment Co.*

> Creativity is necessary for survival in today's environment. All hotels, once you get outside of the truly five-star hotels of the world, are the same; the product varies only in the color of the lobby. To survive, innovation is the key.
>
> *Michael Leven*
> *President*
> *Days Inns*

> Vision and creativity drive our business. It is important for us to grow, therefore it is important for us to be creative.
>
> *Andre S. Tatibouet*
> *President*
> *Aston Hotels & Resorts*

It is the concept that counts, everything else is secondary; whether it's a restaurant, a hotel or a new way to build railroads—it's the creation of the product that brings it to life, the rest is mechanical.

> Robert Burns
> Chairman
> Regent International
> Hotels

If you are going to go out and make ten to twenty times your money, more of that is going to rest on the front of the creative side of things rather than on trying to squeeze things out from an operational standpoint.

> Richard Bradley
> Chairman
> Bradley Holdings Ltd.

My creativity eventually settles on the bottom line. I'm not here on any religious mission. I'm here to make money for the company.

> Stan Bromley
> Regional Vice President
> and General
> Manager
> Four Seasons Hotel
> Washington

Because we are a development company, doing things differently and more creatively than our competitors is the way we make a name for ourselves and a way to generate future business.

> James Rouse
> The Enterprise
> Foundation

The hotel industry is maturing. Competitiveness will intensify over the next decade. New and creative ideas will be required to develop a successful competitive edge over other hotel products.

> Donald Trice
> President
> Interstate Hotels Corp.

Profitability, growth, tapping new segments—these can only be achieved with creativity.

>Charles Mund
>President
>Service Dynamics
>Corp.

Any company that is able to adapt to change constantly is definitely much more apt to secure a piece of business, and maintain it, than one which just works out of a book.

>Linda Schwabe
>Creative Gourmets

In a corporate environment, the creative process is most important since there are already in place very stringent guidelines and policies. The reward is improved profits, better employee benefits, higher return on investment, and further growth. However, if creativity is motivated by greed, then it is misdirected at the expense of shareholders, employees, and even communities in today's environment of leveraged buy-outs.

>Michael W. N. Chiu
>President
>Prima Hotels/Holiday Inn

Creativity is part of enjoyment of life. You think. You tap your inner resources. Adrenalin flows, ideas come, the right questions are asked. Now you are really enjoying your work because you are adding an extra dimension to it. Not every idea is all new. You might have met it floating in the air years ago. Now you have bumped into it, brought it front and center. You gave it a new twist, now it moves in a new direction, perhaps faster, perhaps in a more appealing package, perhaps its time has come. You have just enhanced the quality of your professional contribution to society. That's what life is all about.

>Curt Strand
>Consultant, formerly
> CEO and Director
>Hilton Hotels
>International

The message is clear: Your life in the hospitality industry will be more rewarding, more enjoyable, and more profitable, if you can become more creative.

WHAT IS CREATIVITY AND HOW CAN I GET MORE OF IT?

> Creativity is an end result of a combination of ingredients, including but not limited to inspiration, flexibility, instinct, adaptability, resourcefulness, originality, and "adoptability", which is borrowing from someone else's ideas with appropriate modifications. All of the above combined with a good dosage of risk-taking directly relate to the financial viability of a given business. In my mind creativity is a preamble to entrepreneurship.
>
> *Michael W. N. Chiu*
> *President*
> *Prima Hotels/Holiday Inn*

> Probably the best way to get employees to be creative is to encourage them not to accept the first solution. Encourage them to approach the problem from this angle, from that angle, from some other angle. Don't accept the first solution unless it is so wonderful there is nothing else.
>
> *William V. Eaton*
> *Senior Principal*
> *Cini-Little International*

> Since my properties are extremely diverse in nature and service mainly repeat customers, I need to change and update them and inject fresh thought. For this reason, I am constantly generating new ideas, and I do not take the first idea, ever. Rather, I always keep thinking.
>
> *William Eberhardt*
> *Restaurateur*
> *President*
> *Dining Associates*

People who are creative have more ideas than people who are not creative. That's all there is to it. Creativity is not a mystical power. It is simply the ability to think up lots of ideas. They don't even have to be good ideas. If you invented the nuclear-powered salad bar, people would consider you creative even though they might not think your idea was good. With this in mind, INNovation is designed to teach you first, how to have lots of ideas and second, how to tell which of those ideas are the good ones. Throughout our experience teaching creativity, we have found that if people stick with our techniques until they generate *many* ideas, they almost always come up with at least one they really like. It is fine to come up with 100 bad ideas as long as you come up with 101 ideas.

Coming Up With Ideas

"Coming up with ideas" sounds easy, but "being creative" sounds difficult. Why? Because people can usually come up with a few ideas about anything; but these ideas that come to mind immediately are almost never creative ideas—they are the obvious ideas. Creative people also think of the obvious ideas, but they don't stop there; they keep on thinking until they are out in the uncharted realm of *un*obvious ideas. It is these unobvious ideas that are the creative ones.

Let's jump right into an example. Suppose we are trying to think of ways to serve salad at our restaurant. A few ideas will come to mind easily: in a bowl, in a salad bar, on a plate, in a sandwich. These four ideas are not considered creative because they've been done before. We just reached into our memories and took out these four ideas. But now we're stuck. We've used up the old ideas and now have to start thinking up some new ones. In other words, we have to be creative. What do we do now?

Let's look at what we came up with and how we came up with it:

1. *Salad in a glass.* Whether or not this is a good idea, it is certainly a new one. We have never heard of a salad served in a glass. If we offered salad in a glass at our restaurant, people would consider us creative.

    Where did this idea come from? The process was simple; salad bowls are glass; glass . . . glasses!

2. *Salad in a waffle.* This might not be too appetizing, but it *is* creative.

    Where did this idea come from? Glasses remind us of cut crystal. The cuts in the crystal look similar to the design in waffles. As you will come to see, creativity depends upon one thing reminding you of another thing, even though the logic of these remindings may not always be clear.

3. *Salad in a garden.* Pick your own fresh vegetables in our backyard and we'll make a salad from them.

   This idea came from a more complex process than the preceding ones. Instead of just passively letting ourselves be reminded of things, we asked the question, "Where does salad come from?" The answer was "a garden," so "why not just leave the salad ingredients in the garden?"

   This time we came up with a creative answer to the initial question by asking a different question and seeing how it related.

4. *Salad for Dessert.* This time we asked a question about the way in which salad is usually served and then considered some changes that could be made. Salad is usually served before the main course but what if we served it for dessert? Immediately visions of lettuce-flavored ice cream and salads with chocolate dressings come to mind.

5. *Video Games and Vitamins Instead of Salad*

   Again, we changed the question. We asked the broader question, "What is the purpose of salad?" and decided that salad serves three important purposes:
   1. It is nutritious;
   2. It gives the customer something to do while the main course is being prepared;
   3. It is fun to eat.

Then we decided that we did not need to serve salad in order to accomplish these three things. We could give the customers vitamin pills to take care of number 1, and we could let the customers play video games while waiting for the main course to take care of 2 and 3.

For the moment we aren't interested in whether any of these salad ideas is good, only that we can generate a lot of them. You can see that in order to generate a large number of different kinds of ideas, you have to ask yourself a lot of questions and engage in some complex mental processes. Most of these will generate silly ideas. But if you stick with it for long enough, you will eventually find yourself following a useful and creative path of reasoning that no one has ever followed before. Sometimes you have to follow 100 divergent paths before you find the good one.

The salad example is just an introduction to the sorts of mental processes that lead to creative ideas. In the upcoming chapters we will formally introduce nineteen idea-generating techniques. We are confident that once you have learned the techniques in this book, you will have no problem coming up with 101 creative ways to serve salad. One of these ideas might just make you a salad mogul.

Perhaps the most famous practitioner of the philosophy of having multitudes of ideas was Thomas Edison. Edison said that "invention is two percent inspiration and 98 percent perspiration." In other words, in order to get to the good ideas you have to work hard and test a lot of bad ideas. When looking for the right material to serve as a filament for the lightbulb, Edison tested 750 different materials before he finally employed tungsten, which is used in lightbulbs to this day. It is jokingly said of Edison's trial-and-error method that after inventing the lightbulb the first thing he did was hold it up to his ear and say, "Hello, Watson, can you hear me?"

A WORKING DEFINITION OF CREATIVITY

How do I maintain our competitive position? I think about the business all the time. I do a lot of reading, traveling, and talking to people. I think about the business morning, noon, and night.
J. Willard Marriott, Jr.
President
Marriott Corporation

A creative mind is never turned off. My mind goes eighteen hours a day. I am always thinking about new questions to ask, new ways of doing things. Ideas build on ideas. A fertile mind is one that is constantly trying to improve the question.

Chris Hemmeter
Senior Partner
Hemmeter Investment Co.

As for when I do my thinking, I believe it is more a twenty-four hour a day operation. I find myself always thinking, often when I'm not even trying to, in the shower or driving in my car. Whenever it's quiet and nobody is bothering me, that's when the idea comes to me.

Richard Bradley
Chairman
Bradley Holdings, Ltd.

Imagine that your mind is an enormous room full of little boxes. In each box is one *piece of information* or *one rule* for understanding or operating in the world. In order to think, you are always opening the boxes and putting the contents of different boxes together to form new boxes. *Creativity occurs whenever you unite the contents of two or more boxes, which, as far as you know, have never been united before in anyone's brain.* For example, when Art Fry at the 3M Corporation combined his mental box containing note paper with his mental box for a new adhesive he had invented that would not stick permanently to anything, he introduced the Post-It pad—a creative and extremely useful idea.

Turning to the boxes that contain rules, if you combine your box that contains the rule, "people become happy when they win races" with the box that contains your "disgruntled housekeeping staff," you may come up with the idea of raising the morale of the staff members by having them run a footrace against the portly executive at the company picnic. It may be a silly idea, but it is creative, and it just might help.

Notice that this definition of creativity says that you have been creative whenever you come up with an idea that *you* think is new. It does not matter if it turns out later that someone else thought of it first. The idea was never before in *your* brain, therefore you had a creative thought. Thus, if you had never heard of a salad bar, and you said to yourself, "Eureka! We could put salad in a bar!", then you would have been creative. Of course, if you want the rest of the world to think that you are creative, you had better come up with something really new. Nevertheless, it can be a boost to your confidence in your creative abilities to know that every original thought that *you* have is creative, independent of whether the world will consider it creative.

THE FOUR TOOLS OF CREATIVITY: KEYS, GLUE, REMINDINGS, AND QUESTIONS

This book uses four simple concepts to help explain the mental processes behind creative thought: keys, glue, remindings, and questions. If you understand these concepts you will have a better understanding of what creative thought is, and you will understand why the techniques in this book work.

Keys and Glue

> "Creative phantasy can, in fact, invent nothing new, but can only regroup elements from different sources."
>
> Sigmund Freud

Using the model of the brain as a great room full of boxes of information, we will say that *keys* are what help you open the mental boxes, while *glue* is what helps you unite the contents of these boxes in potentially useful ways.

Your brain already knows how to use keys and glue. Indeed, you employ this theme whenever you think. However, most of the time you use them unconsciously. You don't think about which mental boxes to open—they just open if your mind decides to use that key. Similarly, you don't think about all of the different ways of putting their contents together—they just get put together in whatever order your brain decides to glue them.

In the next three chapters of the book we will be teaching you the creative use of keys and glue. Basically, this means consciously deciding to use the keys to open more boxes, particularly the unobvious boxes, and then gluing the contents of these boxes together in clever and unobvious ways.

Remindings[1]

> Ripping pages from papers and periodicals will provide an idea bank and visual reminder for later follow-up.
>
> Charles Feeney
> Gerard Atkins & Co. Ltd.

> I read many biographies. I like business biographies—fascinating business biographies of people who lived in the 1880–1940 range in terms of their careers. Some of those biographies you would swear are about current events.
>
> Peter Kline
> President
> Harvey Hotels

> I find that, when I read periodicals, the odds are favorable that I would simply "bump into" solutions or opportunities that can be applied to my situation in business. I find that reading triggers ideas, even though the article may be completely remote from the particular situation I connect it to.
>
> Richard Barger
> Chairman
> Barger Hotel Corp.

> I do a lot of traveling. Creativity is often stimulated by getting out and seeing what else is going on in the market place. That gets me thinking of new things, and I get the other people in my group excited about it.
>
> Jim Simonson
> Vice President
> Restaurants Unlimited, Inc.

A thought never enters your consciousness unless something has put it there. That is, you cannot just get the key to one of the boxes in your mind at random—something has to give you the key to that box. Even when you feel as if something has popped into your head for no reason, there is always something (and it may be something unconscious) that

---

[1] The seminal discussion of the importance of remindings in the creative process is Roger Schank's *The Creative Attitude*, Macmillan Publishing Co., New York, 1988.

was responsible for making you have that thought. If you are walking down the street and you suddenly start thinking about wombats, there must have been something—a baseball *bat*, a previous thought that was related to wombats, a past experience that involved wombats—that reminded you of wombats.

Thus the basic currency of thinking is, in simplest terms, the process of one thought reminding you of another thought. Creative thinking depends upon making use of unobvious remindings. This is because an unobvious reminding will generally give you the key to an obvious box or will suggest an obvious way of gluing together the contents of two boxes.

Questions: The Master Tool

"The important thing is never to stop questioning."

Albert Einstein

I'm trying to create an environment where people ask a differernt question, and by asking different questions, they discover a different set of answers and a whole new set of wonderful ideas.

Michael Kay
President
Portman Hotels

The key to creativity is asking a lot of questions—not the whats but the whys.

Donald Strang
President
Strang Corporation

I really believe that the creative things that have happened in my business through the years have come from people taking an idea and listening to what other people have to say about it. They take something that has existed for many years and ask the question "How can we change it to something else?" They are not creating something new, they are just taking something that is already there and coming from a different direction.

Don Berens
Owner
D. P. Berens, Inc.
Specialty Services

To get creativity flowing in an organization, you have to ask a lot of questions. You resolve problems by asking questions; past experience provides the right ones to ask.

Leslie W. Stern
President
L. W. Stern
Associates, Inc.

The most powerful and ubiquitous tool for creativity is the question. In a sense, all creative thought depends upon questions. You don't use a key until you ask yourself which box to open next. You don't use glue until you ask yourself which things to stick together and how. Again, this questioning process usually takes place unconsciously, but if you want to become more creative, the most important thing that you can do is to consciously ask yourself more questions. If you learn to question everything—the big things, the small things, the relevant things, the irrelevant things, the possible things and the impossible things—you will immediately become more creative.

CHAPTER 2

Just You and Your Yellow Pad

Many creative hospitality leaders expressed the opinion that if they can simply spend quiet time away from the office thinking, they are able to produce innovative ideas. Here is a sample of the type of statements these individuals made.

> After hours, I take off my coat and tie and relax in a quiet space for my time to ponder and think. I devote almost every evening to quiet hours of thinking.
>
> *Ichiro Inumaru*
> *President/General*
>   *Manager*
> *Imperial Hotels, Ltd.*

> The development of my creative ideas is a direct function of the extent to which I can withdraw from all the other things that are on my mind and focus my thinking.
>
> *Peter Yesawich*
> *President*
> *Robinson, Yesawich,*
>   *& Pepperdine*

> Creative ideas come to me when I can get away from the day-to-day pressures of business.
>
> *Charles Mund*
> *President*
> *Service Dynamics*
>   *Corp.*

The most creative thinking I do is in the car, in bed, or while taking a shower, just about any place but the office.

> Robert Agnello
> President
> Koala Inns

Creativity is fostered when I can control my own environment, have no constraints; that's when my creativity can be unleashed.

> Leslie W. Stern
> President
> L. W. Stern
>   Associates, Inc.

Creativity often requires that I leave town; my greatest creativity happens normally when I am on airplanes or in hotel rooms where nobody knows where I am and no telephones can ring.

> John Alexander
> President
> The CBORD Group,
>   Inc.

When I work out or run, my head gets cleared up, and I begin to focus on the most important things that I'm trying to resolve. I also get ideas when I'm taking a shower, dressing, or walking along the street when I am removed and all by myself.

> Fred Eydt
> President
> The Watermark
>   Group, Inc.

Everyone knows that one of the best ways to promote clear thinking is to find some private time and space. Creative people know that it is usually not good enough to sit down and "just think about it," because people tend to have set patterns of thinking about things, whereas creativity depends upon pursuing as many patterns of thought as possible. The creativity techniques in this book are intended to help you search for creative ideas in many more ways than you would "just thinking about it."

This chapter introduces those techniques which use only what you already know. Techniques in later chapters will use other people and external stimuli as sources of ideas, but the techniques in this chapter use only the boxes that are ready and waiting in your mind. All you need for Chapter 2 is your yellow pad.

Note that at the heart of the techniques in this chapter are the essential questions:
1. How does this problem or situation relate to other problems or situations I have encountered?
2. How can I change the way it is done now?

TECHNIQUE 1

FREE ASSOCIATION

Creativity is the connecting of ideas. This goes with that, and so on. Be daring. Take the ups and the downs. Have an emotionally true perspective and be true to yourself. Operate in the freedom of self-truth. Creativity is a healthy disease. Hard work plays a role in the process. When people say, "Why?," say to them, "Why not?" It's all how you look at the possibilities and opportunities. Dream.

Joseph H. Baum
President
Joseph Baum & M.
  Whiteman Co.

In order to get ideas, you can't be out to hit a grand slam right off the bat. What managers must realize is that they are going to have to hear 100 to 200 ideas before one or two good ones surface. Once in a while there is a gut feel that you have just heard an idea made of gold, but most of the time there isn't. Ideas have to be combined and messed around with before they work well. Therefore, it is important that you keep your ears open to any idea that you hear; it doesn't make a difference who comes up with it.

Roger Dow
Vice President, Sales
& Marketing
Services
Marriott Hotels and
Resorts

My creative ideas do not come to me when I am at work. My creative ideas come to me when I am in a car, taking a shower, sitting at home watching television, or relaxing; suddenly it comes to me. I am one of those people who gets ideas in the middle of the night. I wake up and I can't go to sleep. So to solve that problem, I keep a pad and pencil next to the bed. I'll write the idea down and go back to sleep.

Jim Petzing
President
CPS Hospitality
Management Ltd.
James E. Petzing &
Associates Inc.

The Free Association technique of idea generation takes advantage of the remindings that occur when you let your mind wander. You start with something (a word, a question, a sketch, a smell, a feeling) that relates to the subject about which you are thinking. Then you let your mind wander and write down the intriguing boxes that it opens.

Suppose, for example, that you are thinking about what sort of entertainment you should use to attract guests to your bar on typically slow Wednesday nights. You start with the word "entertainment."

Entertainment → Movies → Cybil Shephard → An article you read about Cybil Shephard → Magazines → Books → Literary Classics → Sam Shepard → Acting and Writing → The Improvisational Comedy → Aha! Improvisational Comedy. Perfect!

This was a relatively logical reminding pattern. Usually, things are much more random. The randomness might seem like a hindrance, but if you use it correctly, it can turn out to be a source of especially creative ideas. The logical reminding pattern above led to improvisational comedy which, although it is something you might not have thought of, is not enormously creative. Here is a much more "free" free association for solving the same problem:

Entertainment → Movies → Raiders of The Lost Ark → Children → Bubble Gum → Tooth decay → Dental Floss

Now, we have a creative challenge. How can we relate dental floss and entertainment? You could offer a free dental X ray with each drink purchased—nah. You could hire the local dentist to play the drums—nah. Drink discounts for dental technicians. A "best smile" competition. Drink discounts for people who have no cavities. Dental floss dispensers in the rest rooms. Sugarless drink specials.

Silly? Sure, but creative silliness might just be the ticket to a full bar on Wednesday nights.

BRAIN EXERCISES

1. Come up with 25 more ways to glue entertainment and dental floss together.
2. Come up with 25 ways to glue the worst problem that you have in your organization together with the main character on your favorite television show.

TECHNIQUE 2

METAPHORS

Bug spray is like the walls
we build around ourselves.
And like these fragile walls,
It never really works.

       Kate Bergeron, age 14

The young poet saw a metaphorical similarity between bug spray and human defenses. Reading the poem, we learn something about the walls we build around ourselves and perhaps something about bug spray. The poet probably began by opening the "bug spray" box and then was reminded of the key to the "human walls" box. Then she found a way to glue the two together poetically.

Creative people use a lot of metaphors when they think and when they communicate. The lingo of business is replete with metaphors. Here are just a few of them:

Operational Nightmare
Emotional Rollercoaster
Competitive Dogfight
Advertising (Media) Blitz
Financial Drain
Corporate Marriage
Departmental Flagwaving
Cash Shortfall
Negotiation Marathon
Idea Wellspring
Transition Honeymoon
Golden Parachute
Operational Breakthrough
Entering Uncharted Waters

It makes sense that creativity and metaphor would be closely linked. Metaphor is, after all, the revealing of a relationship between two seemingly unrelated things. So if you need some creative ideas, try to think of some creative metaphors. Then think about the metaphorical subject and see if anything that you know about it applies to your initial subject.

For example, suppose that you have the task of updating the computer system in your hotel. You want some creative ideas about how to do this task well. Think of a metaphor for your task. You might come up with: "Updating a computer is like refinishing an old wooden table." Then think about the metaphor and see if anything that you know about the metaphorical subject applies to the initial subject:

1. When you are refinishing an old table, you must repair the flaws in

the wood before you put on the new finish. If you wait until after the finish has dried, it will be too late to do anything about it.
2. Between each coat of finish, you should rub it down with a piece of steel wool.
3. Sometimes an old table is so rotten that you have to throw it out and get a new one.

These three observations are easily translatable to the computer updating task:

Observation 1: I should study the flaws in the old computer system and be certain that the updated system addresses those flaws.

Observation 2: I should test and modify the updated system as it is being installed rather than waiting until it is all done.

Observation 3: Maybe an update is not enough—maybe it would be better to get a whole new system.

By constructing a metaphor with finishing a table, we had some good ideas about updating a computer system.

Once again, if the metaphor gives you the key to a mental box that is seemingly unrelated, you will probably come up with a lot of silly ideas, but you might also come up with one that is even more creative than anything you could have thought of with a more standard metaphor. So if you had said, "Updating a computer system is like eating a cheese puff," you might come up with these observations:
1. Cheese puffs leave orange dust on your hands.
2. Cheese puffs are packed by weight, not volume, so some settling of the contents may occur during shipping.
3. Eating too many cheese puffs can make you sick.

These three observations about cheese puffs would lead to the following observations and questions about computers that you might not have considered if you had not made the metaphor:

Observation 1: How much of the credit for this task is going to rub off on me? This task may leave a lot of work on my hands after the computer experts leave.

Observation 2: How much does the new system weigh? Speaking of "volume," how loud will the new system be? Is it possible to move the system after it has been installed without damaging the contents?

Observation 3: There may be a health risk associated with spending too much time in front of a computer screen. Who will fix the computer if it gets "sick?"

There did not seem to be any "logical" reason why cheese puffs would have anything to do with computers, but in a sense they did. Creativity often results from speculating about the illogical.

BRAIN EXERCISES

1. Construct three more metaphors for the computer updating task: one that is obvious, one that is not so obvious, and one that is outrageous. As with the examples above, you should construct the metaphor, make observations about the metaphorical subject, then apply those observations to the initial subject.
2. This poem was written on the wall of a university rest room:

> *Love is like a snowmobile*
> *Cruising through the tundra.*
> *It flips over and pins you underneath*
> *At night the ice weasels come.*

The meaning of this poem is not obvious. However, if you want to be creative you must learn to leap at any opportunity to explore the unobvious. This poem gives you the keys to a lot of strange and seemingly unrelated boxes. If you can find a way to glue together the contents of these boxes, then you will have some creative ideas. So:
   a. Offer 10 conclusions about love that you can derive from this poem. Don't worry if they are far-fetched. The most creative ideas *are* the "far-fetched" ones.
   b. Change the poem to read:

> My hospitality organization is like a snowmobile
> Cruising through the tundra.
> It flips over and pins me underneath.
> At night the ice weasels come.

    Offer 10 conclusions about your hospitality organization that you can derive from the poem.

c. Think about whatever the poem brings to mind.

Changing The Way It Is

> Creativity, for me, is about challenging the way things are done now—and hopefully coming up with ways that are different and better, at least until you find a better way still. I see creativity as incremental. If you accept and encourage diversity and differences of opinion and build on them, then you allow creativity to bud within the organization.
>
> John Young
Senior Vice President
Human Resources
Four Seasons Hotels

> A creative idea is nothing more than a new way to repackage an existing idea. It's just a different way of looking at an existing problem and it's just recombining the elements in new and different ways. But finding the time to focus on the idea is a big problem.
>
> Peter Yesawich
President
Robinson, Yesawich,
and Pepperdine

Creative people love to change things. This is because they love new ideas—and good ideas tend to change things. So a big step toward becoming a more creative person is to constantly ask yourself such questions as "Why is it like that? How could I change that? What if they did A instead of B? What made them decide to do it that way instead of this way?" Most people only ask such questions about something unusual or something that goes wrong; a creative person asks such questions about everything.

    A creative person *never* accepts the answer "Because that's the way it's always been done." The fast food industry of today is the result of

Ray Kroc's unwillingness to accept that food could only be served in traditional restaurant fashion. Atrium hotels came into existence when John Portman envisioned a hotel lobby different from anything that had ever been attempted. The important first step in changing something is realizing that it does not have to be the way it always has been.

If you ask such questions, you will learn a lot about the world and you may come up with some good ways of improving it. If you question every one of the standard operating procedures in your hospitality organization, you will probably find some that are foolish or outdated or could be improved.

The next four techniques generate ideas by asking variations on the question: "How can I change that?"

TECHNIQUE 3

ATTRIBUTE LISTING

To use the Attribute Listing technique, you list all the attributes of a particular dimension of your hospitality organization, then you consider changes that could be made to each attribute and the implications of those changes.

For example, suppose you want to develop a creative restaurant idea. You would make a list of attributes of a standard restaurant. You should think of as many attributes as you can; we will list just five.

A restaurant:

1. serves food;
2. has waitpersons who bring the food to the customer's table;
3. serves drinks, followed by appetizers and salads, then entrees, and finally desserts;
4. serves the food on plates;
5. gives the customer the check at the end of the meal.

Now you would question and alter each of these attributes:

1. *Serves food* — What if you didn't serve food? You could have a restaurant for dieters who want to go out to a restaurant but don't want to eat. Maybe you would just serve mineral water, celery, and chewing gum. Maybe customers could bring their own food. Maybe . . . What

if you served something other than food? The customer could order a poem or a baseball card du jour. Maybe . . . ?

2. *Waitpersons* What if you didn't have waitpersons? (Maybe it was this question that led to the invention of smorgasbords and fast-food outlets.) You could align the tables along a conveyer belt, and when the customers' orders came up they would just reach over and take them—or you could install revolving "carousels" like they have at the Smithsonian museums in Washington. Or, you could not take orders at all—you could just have a continuous flow of dishes on the conveyer belt and the customer could take whatever looked good. Or, instead of a conveyer belt, you could have a river and float the dishes in wicker baskets. You could drop the food down from the ceiling. What if you let the customer come into the kitchen and get the food? You could . . . What if you had waitpersons but put them on skateboards? What if you had automatons as waitpersons? What if waitpersons sang for the customers? What if . . . ?

3. *Service Order* What if you served the meal backwards: first dessert, then main course, then appetizer, then salad? What if we did it in whatever order the customer requested? What if you only served appetizers? What if you had the waitpersons sing between each course? What if you served all of the courses at once?

4. *On Plates* What if you served the food under the plate? What if you served the food in boxes, baskets, jars? On wooden boards, hubcaps, or some object that suggests the theme of our restaurant? What if you didn't need plates because all food was liquid? What if you put the food directly on the table cloth? What if...?

5. *The Check* What if you let the customer figure out his or her own check? What if you computerized the ordering and check-totalling procedure so that the customer simply typed the order into a computer and the bill was au-

tomatically tabulated? What if you billed the customer's home? What if the customer paid before being served (as in fast-food restaurants)?

As you can see, a simple question about one of the attributes on the list can lead to a profusion of creative ideas. Not only should you apply the attribute listing technique to problems that you want to solve, but also to situations where there is no problem, because it might suggest improvements. In any case, even if it does not lead to any useful ideas for change, attribute listing will teach you a lot about why things are done the way they are done.

BRAIN EXERCISES

1. As in the example above, list five more attributes of the standard restaurant and then question them.
2. Apply the attribute listing technique to a weak aspect of your organization's standard operating procedure.
3. Apply the attribute listing technique to a strong aspect of your organization's standard operating procedure.

TECHNIQUE 4

SCAMPER

I am always trying creative ways of doing things. I do a lot of menu creation at home. For example, last week I tried a new way of cooking vegetables. Instead of undercooking I overcooked them. I overcooked the artichokes until they were crunchy. I overcooked the onions until they were brown. I carmelized the eggplant and cooked the mushrooms until they were really brown. The result was a new flavor, a new characteristic, a new approach. It turned out to be a delicious, thoroughly earthy dish. I also reverse things. I take stuffing and make it a sauce, and I take sauce and make it a stuffing—inside out and outside in—a reversal of elements.

Joyce Goldstein
Owner and Chef
Square One
  Restaurant
San Francisco, CA

In the early 1950s, Alex Osborn, a pioneer in the study of creative thinking, developed a list of action verbs that would lead to the generation of ideas about how to change something. Later, Robert Eberle organized these action verbs into the acronym "SCAMPER":

S = Substitute

C = Combine

A = Adapt

M = Magnify, Minify

P = Put to other uses

E = Eliminate

R = Reverse, Rearrange

If you apply each of these verbs to a procedure or situation that you would like to change, you will come up with some creative ideas.

Consider the traditional check-out procedure in a hotel. How can SCAMPER help us generate ideas for improving the process?

SUBSTITUTE: Check-out by phone, by in-house television channel, by mail; allow check-out at breakfast . . .

COMBINE: Combine check-out payment with check-in; offer breakfast food at check-out location; combine with services for ground transportation; combine with morning work-out at hotel exercise facility . . .

ADAPT: Adapt to the location of the guest; accept more credit cards; adapt to the times that guests want to check-out.

MAGNIFY: Increase the number of people at the check-out desk; make a big production out of check-out so that the guest enjoys it—have trumpets and encourage employees to weep as the guest leaves; have a very large person at the check-out desk so that the guest will be afraid to complain.

MINIFY: Have all forms and bills prepared before the guest comes to check out so that the least amount of time is required; cut some steps out of the current process; computerize to increase speed.

PUT TO
OTHER USES: While the guests are waiting to check out, interview them about their stay and how the hotel could be improved; use check-out time as an opportunity to advertise specials that the hotel will be offering in the future; ask the guests if they wouldn't mind washing some windows for you while waiting to check-out.

ELIMINATE: No check-out—the guest leaves a credit card or a large deposit with you upon arrival so that you don't have to collect money upon departure. Or, do not allow any guests to leave the hotel once they come in—this will significantly increase occupancy.

REVERSE: Come to the guests' room and allow them to check out there; have guests check out when they arrive and check in when they depart (we don't know, you figure it out).

REARRANGE: Rearrange the check-out area; rearrange the procedure for check-out.

A combination of attribute listing and SCAMPER is a particularly effective creativity technique. Make an attribute list and then apply all of the SCAMPER verbs to each element of the list.

BRAIN EXERCISES

1. Apply SCAMPER to the filing procedure in your office.
2. Apply SCAMPER to each attribute in the attribute list that you made in Exercise 2 of the attribute listing section.

TECHNIQUE 5

MATRIX ANALYSIS

The Matrix Analysis technique is a way of ensuring that you open all of the boxes that are directly relevant to a problem. It might lead you to make combinations of boxes which, although they were "right in front of your nose," may never have been considered before.

For example, suppose that your hotel has a cafe which is extremely busy during meals, but is empty between meals. You cannot send the large staff home between meals; you are paying them to do nothing. So you want to think of something that will get people to use the cafe between meals.

With this technique, you set up a matrix which contains one series of related items along a vertical axis and another series of related items along a horizontal axis. Then you fill in the matrix with ideas that relate the vertical items to the horizontal items. In this example, the vertical axis will contain different clientele groups and the horizontal axis will contain different slow periods during the day (Table 2.1).

BRAIN EXERCISES

1. Add some ideas to the above matrix.
2. Set up a matrix that has "ways to make people happy" along the horizontal axis, and "services that my hospitality organization offers" along the vertical axis. Fill in the boxes with as many ideas as you can think of.

TECHNIQUE 6

DESIGN TREE

This technique provides a way to explore how an existing company strength can be applied to other dimensions of a business. You start with the strength (it could be a product, a service, a technology, a staff, a location, a clientele group) and then you draw a "tree" that radiates to the other dimensions of the business that do not take advantage of this strength (Figure 2.1).

TABLE 2.1 Between-meal periods

	Breakfast-Lunch	Lunch-Dinner	Dinner-Evening	Late Night
Young Children	Morning snack and story telling	Afternoon snack and games, crayon drawing, puppet shows	Ice cream, popcorn, Disney movies	Cookies and milk, bedtime stories
Students	Quick between class take-out coffee and snacks	Afternoon snack and study, student-teacher conferences	Late dinner for students who skipped meal plan	Midnight study break, live entertainment, dancing
Tourists	Regional specials, coffee, lecture on local tourist attractions	Local crafts show, regional snacks	Regional desserts, local wine tasting	Update on tomorrow's tourist attractions and events
Business People	Wall St. Journal coffee break	New Age Salad business meeting, after work happy hour with stock closings posted	Dinner for late workers, drinks	A bar for "networking"
Theater Crowd		Early pre-theater dinner	Discount drinks for people who went to really bad shows and walked out	Post-theater munchies
Senior Citizens	Coffee and late breakfast, card games	Snacks, early dinner, lectures or discussions	Dessert coffees, card games, checkers, chess	Ballroom dancing

MATRIX ANALYSIS: Options for increasing use of cafe between meals.

If the strength is a product, you would explore other ways that the product could be used, who else might be interested in the product, how else it might be marketed, and so on.

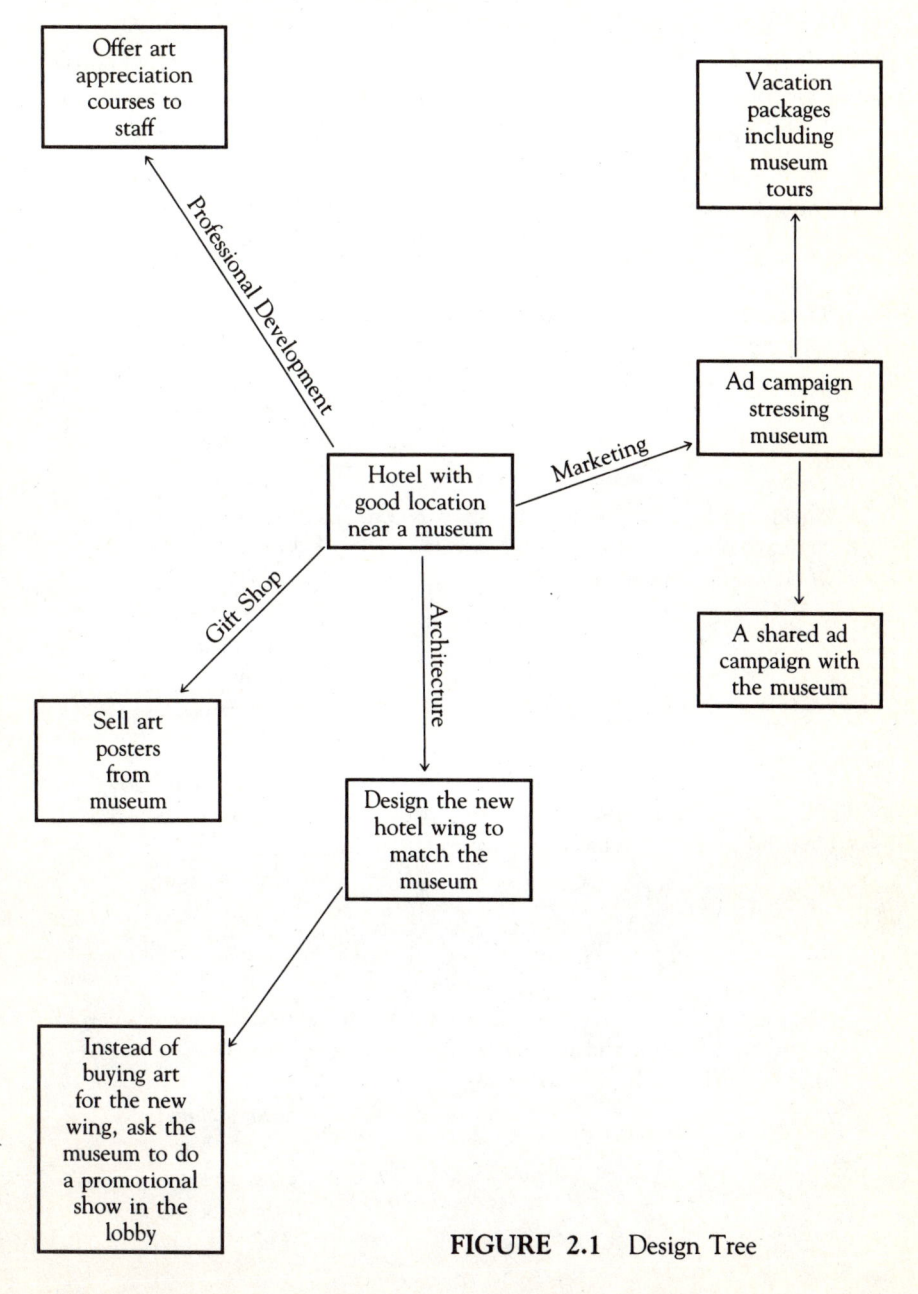

FIGURE 2.1 Design Tree

By the way, before we leave this chapter, it might be appropriate to say a few final words about the yellow pad. The chapter title, "Just You and Your Yellow Pad," suggests that many ideas can be generated with nothing more than your own thoughts and a medium on which to jot, sketch, doodle, draw, or write. However, the little yellow pad carries an additional meaning which may not at first be obvious. It is important that you keep a log of all your ideas even if they do not have any apparent use currently. Keeping a journal of ideas for possible future use is important, as indicated by many of our innovative hospitality leaders.

> I often wake in the middle of the night with a terrific idea; I write down all my thoughts, even the craziest ones, with the hope that I'll still like at least one of them when I wake up in the morning.
>
> Jonathan Tisch
> President
> Loews Hotels

> I keep a pad with me in my car to record all of the ideas which I generate on road trips between my properties; I do my best thinking when behind the wheel.
>
> William Eberhardt
> Restaurateur
> President
> Dining Associates

> I find daydreaming particularly effective, especially when I write down the ideas as they occur to me; this writing process helps to keep the ideas brewing in the back of my mind as well.
>
> Richard W. Barger
> Chairman
> Barger Hotel Corp.

> During the day, I carry a pad in my pocket to write down ideas; even at night, I keep a pad on my bedside so that if I get an idea in the middle of the night, I won't lose it.
>
> Chiaki Tanuma
> Executive Vice
>   President
> Green House Co.,
>   Ltd.

I have started carrying around a tape recorder with me to record ideas.

> H. Etienne Merle
> Chef/Owner
> L'Auberge du Cochon
>   Rouge
> Ithaca, NY

CHAPTER 3

Use a Locksmith

To be creative, you should know about the world: science, medicine, psychology, economics, especially economics. Read and listen. And exercise too. Also, traveling is very stimulating. I am glad that I was able to do so much traveling, and I think everyone should be encouraged to travel. It's an important part of our business.

Curt Strand
Consultant, formerly
CEO and Director
Hilton Hotels
International

I draw from personal experiences with people—friends, former teachers, community and business associates. Everyone has potential to stir creative ideas for my company or at least stimulate thought or open a new outlet.

Michael Leven
President
Days Inns

Biographies are a great source of ideas. Reading about the problems, thought processes, and actions of some of the most brilliant people who have ever lived—what they achieved and how they achieved it—generates insight and inspiration. For example, the lives of Churchill, Gandhi, and Mountbatten (which were intertwined) lead me to re-evaluate myself to ensure that I am making decisions based on sound principles and philosophy.

John Young
Senior Vice President
Human Resources
Four Seasons Hotels

The techniques in this chapter will help you transcend your own personal and organizational boundaries in search of new ideas. You will learn to use outside sources to get access to all kinds of new keys and boxes that will lead you to ideas you could not have come up with on your own. We call these outside sources of ideas *locksmiths* because of their role in helping you get the keys to new boxes.

You will notice that at the heart of all the techniques in this chapter is the question:

How could what I am learning from this locksmith relate to the idea I am looking for?

When we use one of the locksmiths, we are borrowing from another source and applying the idea to our own situation. Our interviews with innovative hospitality leaders lead us to believe that the industry is filled with active borrowers.

> I read about what others have done in similar situations, and I modify and adapt what others have done to best fit my situation.
>
> *Burton Sack*
> *President and CEO*
> *Pub Ventures of New*
>   *England, Inc.*

> Everyone looks at what the competition is doing, what your friend, your colleague is doing.
>
> *Hans Weishaupt*
> *Managing Director*
> *Statler Hotel and*
> *J. W. Marriott*
>   *Conference Center*
> *Cornell University*

> I find myself trying to keep my eyes and ears open for what I think motivates the consumer or would make me anticipate new trends.
>
> *Richard Bradley*
> *Chairman*
> *Bradley Holdings, Ltd.*

I look for something that somebody else is doing in a different discipline which sounds interesting and has application for me.

*Peter Kline
President
Harvey Hotels*

I make a conscious effort to talk to people; the interaction becomes the catalyst to generate the ideas I need.

*G. Michael Hostage
Owner
G. M. Hostage, Inc.*

We pull ideas that have not been tried in our field from various industries, which start the thought process, the "what ifs" and the "why nots."

*William V. Eaton
Senior Vice President
Cini-Little
International*

I am inspired by outstanding people in all different fields. I want to do as well in my own field as they do in theirs.

*Anthony Athanas
Restaurateur
Founder and Owner
Anthony's Pier Four
Boston, MA*

TECHNIQUE 7

LISTS

Lists can be used to grant you easy access to a lot of unobvious connections. They take the place of the "let your mind wander" stage of free association (Technique 1). If the list you choose is not closely related to the subject at hand, you are more likely to find some truly creative ideas.

Suppose you are trying to think of a name for your baby. An obvious locksmith is a naming dictionary. You will not, however, find any creative names in a naming dictionary, because it only includes names that have been used before. A less obvious locksmith would be a nature encyclopedia, which will give you the keys to names such as "Platypus." A mathematical encylopedia would be an even less obvious source of names. It would offer the keys to names such as "Rhombus," "Quadratic," "Slope," and "Pythagoras." Your child may never forgive you, but at least he or she will definitely have a creative name.

The point of using a list as a locksmith is not necessarily to give you the direct solution to your problem, although that may happen sometimes. The point is to open boxes that will make you think, that will make you ask, "How does this relate to my situation?"

A baseball encyclopedia, the phonebook, a list of random numbers, the book of lists are all examples of lists that could be used as locksmiths. It doesn't have to be a list of words. You might see something that gives you an idea in a picture book. Anything that will stretch your mind and grant you access to unobvious boxes is a good list to use as a locksmith.

BRAIN EXERCISES

1. Use the index of this book as a locksmith to give you 101 ideas for the name of a new hotel chain you are starting. The hotel chain caters to people who travel by helicopter.
2. Use the locksmith of your choice as a source of ideas for dealing with a rude employee.

TECHNIQUE 8

TRIED AND TRUE LOCKSMITHS: PROVERBS

In our definition of creativity, we suggested that one source of creative ideas is gluing the contents of a box that contains a rule for understanding and operating in the world to the contents of other boxes in original ways. For example, if you take the rule that says, "always eat the middle of an Oreo before eating the two cookies" and apply it to the box that contains peanut butter and jelly sandwiches, you will come up with a creative way of eating the peanut butter and jelly before eating the bread.

Roger Schank suggests that proverbs are an excellent example of such rules for understanding or operating in the world.[2] Schank refers to such rules as *explanation patterns*, or XPs. He maintains that proverbs

---

[2] Roger Schank, *The Creative Attitude*, Chapter 8, p. 222 or 225.

not only reflect the tried and true wisdom of our culture, but that they also reflect the way our brains are organized. He has therefore developed the following technique of using proverbs as locksmiths.[3]

Suppose you are trying to increase the number of repeat guests at your hotel. Using this technique the first step is to look in a book of proverbs under some of the headings that relate to this problem. The following proverbs are found under the headings of "hospitality," repeating, "guests," and "friendship":

1. Short visits make long friends.
2. The tree does not withdraw its shade even from the woodcutter.
3. Hospitality consists in a little fire, a little food, and an immense quiet.
4. In times of prosperity, friends will be plenty; in times of adversity, not one amongst twenty.
5. Friendship is a plant which must often be watered.

The next step in the process is to translate the proverb into neutral terms. Thus, the translated proverbs would read:

1. People enjoy short visits more than long visits.
2. It is important to be hospitable to everyone, even if they are not kind to you.
3. Peace and quiet are an important part of hospitality.
4. Friendships are easier to maintain when the friends are prosperous.
5. A friendship must be maintained if it is to grow.

The third step is to relate the sound advice in these proverbs to your own situation.

1. The first proverb might suggest that you should have short weekend specials and one-night specials. These will entice your customers to come back again because they have not had time for the full experience of your hotel.
2. The second proverb might suggest that your staff is not sufficiently trained in dealing with difficult guests. Maybe if they learned to accommodate such guests, the guests would become repeat customers.
3. The third proverb suggests that maybe the secret of making people

---
[3] *Ibid.*, Chapter 8, pp. 222–250.

return is to create such a placid atmosphere in your hotel that guests will associate your hotel with relaxation and peace.
4. The fourth proverb suggests that part of the issue might be to convince your guests that they are prosperous enough to deserve your hotel. Perhaps you can advertise the ways in which a stay in your hotel could actually lead to greater prosperity.
5. The final proverb might suggest that you need to spend more time "watering" the friendships you have with your customers. Maybe you should call them once a month just to see how they are doing. Maybe you should send Season's Greetings cards, birthday cards, flowers.

One important thing to keep in mind when using proverbs as locksmiths is that the advice contained in them is not the law. In fact, for most proverbs there is another proverb that contradicts it. For every "too many cooks spoil the broth" there is a "two heads are better than one." Proverb number four in the list above is contradicted by "misery loves company." Proverbs one and five partially contradict each other.

Why is the tried and true wisdom in proverbs so full of contradictions? Well, proverbs became proverbs because they helped people deal with the difficult questions in life—the questions to which there are no right answers. This is why proverbs can be so beneficial to the creative process. Because they relate to questions for which there are no right answers, they lead us to subjects in which there is lots of room for creativity. If there is no best answer, there is always a need to think of new and better answers.

The Fortune Cookie Meeting

The fortune cookie meeting is a format for an enjoyable and surprisingly effective creative meeting. Bring a bag of fortune cookies and pass a few cookies out to each person. Then, using Technique 8 (Proverbs), apply the fortunes in the cookies to the issue that you are discussing. Even when the fortune seems to be unrelated to the question at hand, find a way to relate it. Fortune cookies tend to contain proverbs and other "rules for dealing with the world" and, as such, serve as excellent proverbial locksmiths.

TECHNIQUE 9

INNOVATIVE IMITATION[4]

Creative imitation is the source of most of my "new" ideas.
Charles F. Feeney
Gerard Atkins & Co. Ltd.

One of the best locksmiths available is another organization. Go scout your competitors. Go learn about organizations in other industries that have been successful in similar situations. Sometimes you will be able to import an idea in its entirety from one of these organizations. What is even better is when you can see a missing ingredient in the other organization's idea which, if added to the idea, would be the key to your organization's success. You should also look at ideas that failed in other organizations. Failure is a crucial source of creative ideas. From learning about these failures, you not only learn to avoid failure in your organization, but you also might be able to see that missing ingredient that would turn that failure into a success.

There is nothing unethical about innovative imitation, and even though it involves "borrowing" other people's ideas, it is still creative because you will refine the idea for use in a new situation.

> Creative imitation is not "innovation" in the sense in which the term is most commonly understood. The creative imitator does not invent a product or service; he perfects and positions it. In the form in which it has been introduced, it lacks something. It may be additional product features. It may be segmentation of product or services so that slightly different versions fit slightly different markets. It might be proper positioning of the product in the market. Or the creative imitation supplies something that is still lacking.[5]

---

[4] Peter Drucker, "Entrepreneurial Strategies," *California Management Review*, Winter 1985, pp. 9–25. (The term "creative imitation" was coined by Theodore Levitt of the Harvard Business School.)

[5] Peter F. Drucker, *Innovation and Entrepreneurship: Practices and Principles*, Harper & Row, New York, 1985, p. 206.

TECHNIQUE 10
LEARN ABOUT SOMETHING ELSE

A surprising number of scientific discoveries are made by scientists studying in fields other than their own. This is probably because the knowledge and methods these scientists acquired in their initial fields allow them to see the new field in a way that no one else has looked at it.

If you want to bring a creative outlook to your hospitality organization, you should learn a lot about some other subject and then try to apply that body of knowledge to your organization.

Creative people have a thirst for knowledge of all sorts. What is the state of the art in bee farming? How do eskimos treat the elderly? What questions are physicists asking today? How do baseball players train? Why did grass become the desirable plant to have in lawns? The creative person realizes that the answer to any of these questions might someday be applicable to a problem that needs a creative solution. In addition to their general curiosity about life, creative people often have one subject of interest that they study in great depth.

Take for instance Carmel D'Arienzo, a New York City native of Italian extraction. As a college student she *spent* a great deal of *time in Italy* on part-time jobs and extended vacations, and came to know and love her country of origin. Carmel also *loved to bake*. She learned that Italy lacked chocolate chip cookies, so after completing graduate studies in hotel & restaurant administration, she moved to Florence, Italy and set up her own business selling chocolate chip cookies. Two years later Carmel's Cookies is flourishing and even stays open between 1:30 and 3:30 PM when most other local businesses close down. Thus Carmel D'Arienzo was able to combine a New Yorker's knowledge of chocolate chip cookies to her awareness of a potential market for them in Italy.

So learn about other things and then ask yourself, "How does that relate to the hospitality industry?"

TECHNIQUE 11

LET EMPLOYEES AND STAFF KNOW THAT YOU AND YOUR ORGANIZATION ARE EAGER FOR CHANGE

Not only should you be eager to question and make changes, but you should also let everyone else know that they should be doing the same. An organization that asks for ideas will get them.

Too often managers feel that because they are in charge, they must conceive all ideas and make all changes. For example, they ponder how they can make the housekeeping staff more efficient but never ask the experts on the subject, the members of the housekeeping staff.

Ask every employee how he thinks he could do his own job better. Ask every employee how you could do your job better. Let every employee know that you are interested in any ideas about how the organization could be improved.

In *The Creative Corporation*, Karl Albrecht suggests that every corporation should adopt the rule, "You are authorized to think." [6] Employees are thrilled by the opportunity to contribute ideas. They also respond to their own ideas with more enthusiasm than to ideas that are imposed upon them.

Before leaving our discussion of locksmiths, it seems wise to note that the best locksmith in the world will not help you if you are not willing or able to be a good observer and listener. Customers will serve as locksmiths if you will simply observe them. You must see and hear what is going on around you in order to take advantage of the locksmiths that continually pervade your surroundings. Innovative industry leaders recognize the importance of being aware.

> To be creative, you have to be aware of what is going on around you and file it in your clever-idea file, which acts as fuel to feed the creative process.
>
> H. Jay Sloofman
> President
> Marketing Visions,
> Inc.

---

[6] Karl Albrecht, *The Creative Corporation*, Dow Jones-Irwin, Homewood, IL, 1987, p. 32.

To be creative, you have to be a good observer. People will give you thousands of creative ideas; all you have to do is listen and watch.

> Hans B. Bremstrom
> President
> Sara Hotels
>   Management Corp.

Understanding one's customers is critical; I think about my guests in terms of giving them an experience that exceeds their expectations.

> Jane B. Tatibouet
> Vice President
> Human Resources
> Aston Hotels &
>   Resorts

You cannot make strategic decisions unless you have a deep understanding and heavy personal involvement. You have to be able to think things through and be a good listener.

> J. Willard Marriott, Jr.
> President
> Marriott Corporation

We have to understand people; once we understand people, then we can be responsive to people, and we have started the creative process.

> Chris Hemmeter
> Senior Partner
> Hemmeter Investment Co.

For a creative person, everything in the world is a locksmith. A creative person keeps all five senses on the alert for an input that could spark an idea.

It is important to see all of the elements and feel through all of the senses, and then something will come about.

> Alice Waters
> Chef/Owner
> Chez Panisse

Honing all your senses is important in the hotel industry: touch, taste, smell, sight, hearing. Each aspect plays an important role in the entire guest experience.

Michael Leven
President
Days Inns

I try to expose myself to many different situations and experiences and many different people. I try to involve as many senses as possible.

H. Etienne Merle
Chef/Owner
L'Auberge du Cochon
  Rouge
Ithaca, NY

CHAPTER 4

How Could the Question Be Changed?

> I can't stress enough the importance of asking questions. By simply asking a question, you can make the unfamiliar familiar. Questions like "what?" help to build understanding. It helps a person gain insights on the habits of the user, the advantages and disadvantages, and what problems you could expect. "Why" could help you determine why people want it or use it. "When?" could help you consider the time for its use and its relationships to other things.
>
> Robert Colombo
> General Manager
> Grand Hyatt Hotel
> New York

As you may have noticed by now, many good ideas are generated by changing the question that is being asked. For example, when the initial question was "What should be the theme of my new restaurant?", we applied the attribute listing technique to change the question to a series of questions: "What sort of food should I serve?", "How should the food get to the customers?", "What if we don't use plates?"

If you are having trouble coming up with creative answers to a question, it could be because you are trying to answer an unanswerable question or because too many people have asked that question for you to think of anything new. In such situations, you should change the question.

This chapter contains eight techniques for changing the question. They can be applied to any question, however, here we will apply them to the question "How can my organization make more money this quarter?"

TECHNIQUE 12

QUESTION BREAKDOWN

Question breakdown is just like attribute listing except that it is applied to a question instead of to a facet of an organization. Each word of the question is analyzed and possible alterations are considered. We take apart the sample question as follows:

HOW   Before we ask "how," maybe we should ask "Why—Why do we want to make more money?" Are we looking for a "how" that will pay off immediately or at the end of the quarter? What does it mean to make more money? Where are we going to make this money? What will be the cost of making this money?

CAN   Can we make more money or is that impossible? If I collected the five cent deposit on every *can* of soda that our organization drinks, would that make enough money for us?

WE   Maybe "we" aren't the ones who should be making this money; maybe another part of the organization should be responsible. Who is "we?" Is it just the management or is it everyone? Do we all want to make more money or is it just some of us? Who is the most eager to make more money? Is there a change we can make in who "we" are that would help us make money? Whose money will we be acquiring?

MAKE   What are the different ways of making money? Should we just make it and keep it or should be invest it or spend it?

MORE   How much more money? Is more better than less? Could we make the same amount of money and then use it more efficiently? Can we get Mary Tyler Moore involved?

MONEY   Is money what we want more of? Maybe we really want more fame, more love, more time. What kind of money—

dollars, pounds, lire, yen? What is likely to happen in the financial world this quarter that might affect our attempt to get more money?

THIS Is it really *this* quarter that we should try to make more money? Maybe it would be wiser to make the money during another quarter.

QUARTER Is a quarter a realistic time frame? Maybe we should plan to make more money this decade. Can we make more money in quarters by installing video games and slot machines?

Just analyzing the words that compose a question will lead you to a wealth of new and possibly better questions. It also gives you a much deeper understanding of the initial question.

TECHNIQUE 13

ASK BROADER OR NARROWER QUESTIONS

In order to reach a creative solution to a problem, it is important to have a clear definition of just what that problem is. Sometimes what we perceive a problem to be is not the problem at all. Although all problem solvers face the necessity of carefully defining the problem at hand, consultants run a particular risk of being hired to solve a problem that may have been ill-defined for them.

> One of the most challenging creative needs of a consultant is to be able to confirm or redefine the perceived problem. An example of this need might be that the weak interpersonal skills of top management are creating organizational problems resulting in unsuccessful marketing strategies. The management may consider engaging a consultant, but his definition of the problem will more likely than not be something other than his own interpersonal skills. A common situation is that top management is autocratic and does not seek the benefit of middle management's understanding of the customer. If the decision maker's lack of understanding of the customer results in low market share or failure of a product line, top management may define the problem as one of marketing. The consultant needs to find an approach to work with the prospective client to confirm, clarify, or, more typically, re-

define the problem. The consultant not only needs to remain independent but must quickly develop an understanding of the environment. The consultant is a player receiving incomplete and possibly misleading information while trying to solve a complex puzzle. There are also the challenges of "selling" a redefinition of the problem if necessary and then "selling" proposed solutions.

Bjorn Hanson
Managing Director
Laventhol & Horwath

Sometimes it helps to change the scope of a question. If you ask "How can I achieve world peace?", you may be asking too broad a question. However, if you ask "How can I stop this soldier from shooting that soldier?", your question may be too narrow.

Experiment with the scope of your questions. Broader versions of our sample question include:

- Why do we want more money this quarter?
- How can we make more money this decade?
- How can we be more successful?
- What is money?
- How can the nation's economy be improved?
- How can the world's economy become more prosperous?

Narrower versions of our sample question include:

- How can we increase our profits by eleven percent this quarter?
- How can breakfasts be more profitable in the restaurant this quarter?
- How can we cut costs today?

TECHNIQUE 14

ASK THE QUESTION OF A METAPHOR

In Chapter 1 we used metaphors to shed new light on a problem. In this chapter we will use metaphors to change the question. To apply this technique, take the question and ask it about something else with which it shares a metaphorical relationship.

For example, we could say there is a metaphorical relationship between making more money this quarter and making more friends this quarter. Both require hard work, luck, and commitment; both can be lost if mishandled, and both can lose their value. So we might re-ask our sample question as "How would we make more friends this quarter?" Among the answers we might come up with are:

- Make ourselves more visible at social occasions.
- Be more friendly.
- Be less selfish.
- Pursue hobbies that friendly people pursue.
- Give people gifts and money.

As you can see, these are effective ways of making friends, but they are easily transformable into effective ways of making money. The metaphors were the key to a series of boxes related to friendship that we might not have opened if we had only opened boxes related to money.

You should also construct metaphors between the current situation and experiences in your past. Thus another important question to ask is: How did I make more money last time?

TECHNIQUE 15

ASK OPPOSITE QUESTIONS AND INSIDE-OUT QUESTIONS

No matter what the question is, it is always interesting and often fruitful to ask the opposite question. If the question is "How can we achieve world peace?", ask "How would we achieve world war?" If the question is "How can we make more money?", ask "How can we make less money?"

Often such opposite questions require creative answers. You have never learned how to intentionally make less money. The creative answers that you supply to these questions may shed some light on the initial question.

Inside-out questions serve a similar purpose. In this case, one of the inside-out questions is "How can money make more we?", or, correcting the grammar, "How can money make more of us?" This leads to the idea of expanding the company. Another inside-out question is "How can more of us make money?" This leads to the idea of improving per capita productivity.

TECHNIQUE 16

ASK PRECEDENCE AND CONSEQUENCE QUESTIONS

In his book *The Creative Attitude*,[7] Roger Schank refers to two important ways of re-asking questions as "Precedence Tracking" and "Consequence Following."

Precedence-tracking questions inquire about the events and motives that preceded the current question. The precedence-tracking questions might be:

- What events led up to our desire to make more money?
- What is the origin of desire?
- What is the origin of money?
- What made our economy the way it is?

Consequence-following questions inquire about the consequences of decisions. The consequence-following questions in this case might be:

- What will happen to us if we make more money?
- What will happen to the organization if we make more money?
- What will happen to employee morale if we make more money by cutting salaries?
- What will we do if at the end of the quarter we have not made more money?

TECHNIQUE 17

ASK THE "REAL" QUESTION

I try to encourage a customer orientation in all that we do. We have a strong research department that is asking the questions, "What is going on in the customers' minds?" "Who is traveling and why?" "What experiences do they want?" We have smart people who interpret the research. Research is expensive, but it is the way we can take the pulse of the customer. The speed of change continues to accelerate. We have to have ideas cooking constantly.

> J. Willard Marriott, Jr.
> President
> Marriott Corporation

---

[7] Roger Schank, *The Creative Attitude*, Macmillan Publishing Co., NY, 1988, pp. 292–293.

We put ourselves in the customers' place and ask what is it that the customer wants. Bathrobes! Everyone thought we were crazy. But the reason we did it was that customers do not want to carry a lot of baggage. Wouldn't it be nice to have a fluffy, comfortable bathrobe in the room? Other things which we thought the business traveler would find convenient are hairdryers and overnight pressing and shoeshine. You can feel confident traveling with one suit and one pair of shoes if you have these services. They are very widely used services. With them, customers leave with a feeling of value added.

Another problem with hotel rooms is the shortage of space. How can you take the existing room and improve the space? You certainly can't take out the bed or dresser. We were concerned with how we could get rid of the typical line of furniture along the wall in the room and make it more residential in feeling. We developed the armoire to house the television and bought residential rather than hotel furniture. The armoire killed two birds with one stone. It is residential in character, and it also provided the greatest "luxury" of all—space!

We are constantly trying to get into our customer's mind and refine and re-define our services accordingly.

John L. Sharpe
Executive Vice
President
Four Seasons Hotels

I'll ask customers what they want to see in a hotel. They'll tell me everything I want to hear. But then I'll go back and say, "Tell me about your stay last night. What was wrong with your stay?" Then they will just take off; they will tell me all the things that went wrong. Now the challenge is how to quantify those wrongs. Some things are inconveniences and other things are real big problems.

Peter Yesawich
President
Robinson, Yesawich,
and Pepperdine

Sometimes people do not ask the question that they really want to ask. For example, if the question is "Should I let the bar make an extra $10,000?", the answer is "yes" until the bartender explains that the money will be made by selling liquor to twelve-year-olds. Similarly, a person will say that what he wants is to make an extra $10,000 this year, when all he really wants is to impress his friends. Roger Schank suggests that in such situations one must ask "goal precedence" and "target directed" questions.

Goal precedence questions ask "what other goals or values will be sacrificed in the pursuit of the goal in question." In the preceding example, the question really is "Does my goal of making more money take precedence over my goal of not selling liquor to minors?"

Target-directed questions ask "What is really wanted?" The target-directed question in this case is, "Do I really want to make an additional $10,000 or am I just trying to impress my friends? If I am just trying to impress my friends, is there a better way I could do that?"

TECHNIQUE 18
ASK THIS LIST OF QUESTIONS

Roger Schank has composed a list of the questions that people tend to ask about objects and actions.[8] The questions can be asked in any situation. Sometimes, certain questions will seem foolish and irrelevant when applied to a particular issue; but often these are the questions that lead to the most creative ideas. For example, from using Schank's list below we would get the question, "What would go inside money?" This may not make sense, but it does start you thinking.

Object Rules

1. *Where From*
   Where did you get an X?
   Is it difficult to find an X?
2. *Function*
   What do you do with an X?
   Why would someone want an X?
3. *Enablement*
   How did you manage to get an X?
   How did you get the resources to get an X?
4. *Habits*
   Are you in the habit of Xing?

---
[8] *Ibid.*, pp. 254–256.

How does having an X fit in with other behaviors?
Is this the start of a new trend with things like X?
5. *Associated Objects*
What would go inside that X?
What goes with that X?
What does the X go in?
6. *Results*
What did you do with the old X?
How do you like being in state Y that results from using X?
7. *Problems*
Might it not be a problem to have an X?
What does having an X say about you?
Is it difficult to keep your X?

Action Rules

1. *Next Event*
   What happened next?
   What usually happens next?
2. *Preceding and Enabling Events*
   How did you happen to be Xing?
   What led up to Xing?
   How were you able to X?
3. *Associated Objects*
   How were you able to X without a Y?
   Whom did he X with?
   Where did he X?
   How did you get a Y that enabled you to X?
   What did you X with?
4. *Other Actors*
   Who else Xes?
5. *Associated Actions*
   What other actions usually go along with Xing?
6. *Physical Results*
   Do you want state Z to come from Xing?
   Why would one want Z to be the case?

How does Z help the actor?
Who else does Z benefit?
7. *Scripts*
What patterns of actions must have been occurring?
What else was going on?
8. *Reason*
Why did X take place?
9. *Alternative Plans*
Why wasn't Z done instead?
What other action achieves the same aims?
Why do people make the choices they do?
What are the side effects of the chosen plan or its alternatives?
10. *History*
What was going on when you heard about X?
How often does X occur?
What causes things like X in general?
11. *Mental or Social Effect*
Did you like Xing?
What difference does Xing make?
What would happen if everybody Xed?

We would like to add to Schank's list the following questions:

- How does the competition do it?
- Could we computerize it?
- Is it my fault?
- What is the meaning of X?
- How long will X last?
- How will they do X in the future?
- In 25 years, where will this leave you? In 100 years?
- How will people feel about X?

TECHNIQUE 19

ASK RIDICULOUS QUESTIONS

Sometimes creativity comes from asking ridiculous questions. The list below contains a few of our favorites. Most of the time they will yield ridiculous answers, but occasionally they just might lead to something novel and useful. We have found that people are often pleasantly surprised by the ideas that these questions generate.

1. What would happen if X could fly?
2. What would happen if we tried this underwater?
3. Do I know any relevant proverbs or jokes?
4. Does my favorite cartoon have anything to do with this? My favorite song?
5. What would my mother think? What would my best friend think? What would my clergyman think?
6. How many roads must a man walk down before he can X?
7. Could we make this more humorous? More beautiful?
8. How could food be involved? Music? Sex? Nature? Velcro?
9. What questions would a four-year-old child ask in this situation?
10. How would a four-year-old child behave in this situation?
11. What does this have to do with the values of my generation? The values of my organization?
12. What would happen if we turned it upside-down? Inside-out?
13. How can we pretend X is something else?
14. What color should we use?
15. What should it taste like? Smell like? Feel like? Sound like?
16. If I had unlimited time and money, how would I do it?
17. Where will this end?

CONCLUSION

In Chapters 2, 3, and 4 we introduced nineteen techniques that aid in the generation of new ideas. We learned that creativity is the result of asking questions, opening boxes, and gluing the contents of boxes together in original ways. You should feel confident that as long as you are willing to employ these techniques, you will always be able to come up with 101 ideas, no matter what the problem is you are trying to solve. Frequent use of the nineteen techniques will also get your brain in the habit of thinking creatively, even when you are not consciously employing the techniques.

CHAPTER 5

The Creative Group—How to Make More Heads Better Than One

Let people develop their own ideas. Give them the freedom to do this. Push down in the organization as far as possible the notion of letting people develop their own ideas. It is important not to stifle an idea. I try not to say "no" to new ideas; rather I try to encourage new ideas. I let them run with it. Reward employees when they get a good idea.

>J. Willard Marriott,
>Jr.
>President
>Marriott Corporation

Within staff groups, it is necessary to have both right- and left-brain thinkers. Sometimes it can get a bit tense, but all groups need idea creators, idea organizers, and idea implementors.

>Michael Leven
>President
>Days Inns

I like to have people with different perspectives on my staff. I don't want everybody who thinks the same way I do. I want people who are smarter than I am.

>Andre S. Tatibouet
>President
>Aston Hotels &
>   Resorts

A great deal of the thinking and planning done by most organizations takes place in meetings. Thus, if an organization is to become more creative, it must promote creativity in groups. In this chapter we will discuss the best ways of leading a group to a good idea.

One of the keys to developing creative groups is the inspiration of a team concept among the participants. Many innovative industry leaders expressed their beliefs that interaction with others stimulated the creative process.

> Creativity is stimulated by interaction.
>
> Leslie W. Stern
> President
> L. W. Stern Associates, Inc.

> I believe that a group environment is a great place to encourage creative thoughts. People get creative in the context of bouncing ideas off other people.
>
> Michael Kay
> President
> Portman Hotels

> When I share an idea with others and listen to their suggestions, the idea will always be improved by whatever restrictions or enlargements they can give me.
>
> J. William Keithan
> Former Senior Vice President
> Westin Hotels and Resorts

> People who feel comfortable with their surroundings and with their fellow workers come up with good ideas; the ability to communicate and cooperate is vitally important.
>
> John Mariani
> Chairman
> Banfi Vintners

I think the greatest creativity in the world is probably the total of a lot of interested committed people.

> Donald Berens
> Owner
> D. P. Berens Inc.
> Specialty Services

Theoretically, a group should be extremely creative. The more people there are to think about something, the more boxes can be opened and the more types of glue can be supplied. In practice, however, groups often fail to live up to their creative potential. People in groups are embarrassed to share their bad ideas. They are afraid to share a bad idea for fear that others will think they are stupid. This fear is a serious hindrance to the group's creative process. As we have seen in the previous chapters, the best creative ideas often spring from the bad ideas. If people are not sharing their bad ideas, a crucial source of good ideas has been lost. Thus one of the important subjects discussed in this chapter concerns how to rid people of their inhibitions about sharing bad ideas.

> You have to create the climate for creativity. Let's face it, the guy that owns the restaurant isn't the only guy who has to be creative. What you are really going to have to do, I think, is set the climate within an organization. Ideas are anywhere in the organization, and I think you can put a little framework to it. Creativity isn't something where you just walk around and all of a sudden the light bulb goes on. Creativity is hard work, and it comes from a structure. In an organization, I think it is important that we create a structure—maybe you pose a problem, an objective, a challenge for a group of employees. You must be willing to invest their time in the project of being creative.
>
> Richard Ferris
> Former President
> United Airlines

THE SPEECH

Before any group is asked to do something creative, it should be given a version of The Speech. The Speech is a way of ridding people of their inhibitions about sharing bad ideas. This is what the speech should say:

"We are now going to try to (whatever the creative thing is you are trying to do). This is going to require some creative thought. I want to remind everyone that good creative ideas do not appear easily or quickly. They require a lot of thinking. So we are now going to try to generate a lot of ideas. Most of these ideas will be silly. That is *good*! We want silly ideas. Often the best creative ideas are the result of modifying a silly idea. So if you have a silly or foolish idea, share it! If you have a dumb question, ask it! We won't think that you are silly or foolish. We will think that you are making an essential contribution to the creative process."

DISCUSSION FORMATS

Once you have given The Speech, you should next introduce the discussion format that will be used. A discussion format is a procedure that the group will follow as it searches for ideas. The discussion formats that we will introduce in this book are Group Brainstorming, the Nominal Group Technique, NGT-Storming, and Question Questing.

Discussion Format #1: *Group Brainstorming*

In the group brainstorming discussion format, the members of the group are encouraged to generate ideas in a rapid-fire, free-flowing manner. No one leads the discussion. The idea is to quickly get the keys to a lot of mental boxes. A fast note-taker should be used to keep a record of everything that comes up in the discussion, preferably on something large enough for all to see. Five rules must be followed:

1. *No Judging* No criticisms or judgments should be made about anything that anyone says. Never say, "Let's get down to earth" or "let's not be ridiculous" or "that's stupid."
2. *Encourage Freewheeling* As you will have explained in The Speech, no idea is too absurd to mention. The general feeling should be that the wilder it is the better, because it will open up new paths of thought.
3. *Go For Quantity* As usual, the goal is to come up with as many ideas as possible. Do not allow any lulls in the conversation, keep the ideas flowing fast and furiously (see rule 5).
4. *Encourage Piggybacking* If an interesting idea comes up, feel free to

"piggyback" on it; modify it, pursue it further, ask new questions about it.

5. *Ask Questions*   The contributions to the brainstorming session should be both ideas and questions. When there is a lull in the discussion, a provocative question can be perfect for generating new discussion. Use the eight question-changing techniques presented in Chapter 4.

Once an extensive list of ideas and questions to consider has been developed, the ban on judging is lifted and the group reviews the list. At this stage, the group should be more practical and try to converge upon a few ideas and questions it wants to consider more deeply.

What follows is a transcript of the beginning of a hypothetical brainstorming session:

Jane: Ok team, lets brainstorm names for our new fast-food restaurant which features low-sodium foods.

Jill: Something that points out that the food will be good for your heart, cold hands—warm heart, Sweet Hearts, Big Hearts—

Ted: Heart warming, Open Hearts, No Heart Breaker—

Jane: No Salt Shaker, No Heart Breaker—

Glen: How about something using heart and hearth?

Jill: The Warm Hearth, Hearth and Soul—

Ted: Food with Heart—

Glen: Hearty Food. . . Listen to your heart, An Affair of the Heart—

Jill: The Hearty Hearth—

(there is a brief lull in the conversation, Jane re-kindles discussion with a question)

Jane: Besides being good for your heart, what are the other benefits of low-sodium food?

Jill: It isn't excessively salty, you can taste the other spices

Glen: Low Salt, High Taste, Saltaholics Anonymous,

Ted: Taste 'n Pepper

Jane: The atomic symbol for Sodium is Na. How about NoNa?

Jill: Low Na, BaNaNa—

Jane: We have the beginnings of some great names. How can we combine the three strengths: good for your heart, more interesting to taste, and fast?

Ted: Great Heart, Head Start, Taste Art . . . etc.

There are no particularly good names in this brief transcript. Indeed, some of the ideas are horrible. For example, "Open Heart," with its suggestions of surgery, would be an embarrassing name for a restaurant that is supposed to be good for your heart. Still, no one passed judgment on the bad ideas. Instead, they concentrated on generating new ideas.

Jane's group does not have the right name yet, but we can be confident that by the time they have thought of one hundred names they will have thought of at least one that they like.

Applying the Creativity Techniques in a Brainstorming Session

The techniques we have introduced in the previous three chapters work not only for individuals, but also for groups. Groups that are brainstorming can significantly increase the quantity and quality of their ideas if they use these techniques. We have found the most effective techniques for group brainstorming to be:

1. Free association
2. Locksmiths
3. Attribute Listing
4. SCAMPER
5. SCAMPER + Attribute Listing
6. Matrix Analysis
7. Design Tree
8. Question Breakdown

We recommend that you first let the brainstorming session take its natural course; then, when things slow down, utilize one of the techniques.

Discussion Format #2: *The Nominal Group Technique (NGT)*

The *Nominal Group Technique* consists of six steps. The first three require divergent thinking (idea generation) and the last three require convergent thinking (idea selection). We will discuss the subject of idea selection in more depth in Chapter 6.

Step 1. The group members work individually. For five to twenty minutes, each person works on generating a list of ideas and questions. If the subject for discussion has been introduced before the meeting, then people can be encouraged to come to the meeting with their lists already prepared. Participants should use the techniques in the previous chapters during Step 1 of the NGT.

Step 2. The participants begin to function as a group. The group leader goes around the table eliciting a single idea from each of the participants, while a recorder lists the ideas on a large sheet of paper or chalk board. After each person has contributed an idea, the leader again goes around the table taking a second idea from each participant. The leader keeps going around until everyone is out of ideas.

Step 3. Each idea which has been recorded is discussed by the group. Questions may be asked, modifications may be suggested, problems with the idea may be pointed out, but no qualitative judgments such as "this idea is great" or "this idea is dumb" should be made.

Step 4. The participants individually rank the ideas. If there are fifty ideas, each participant's favorite idea would be ranked 1 and the least favorite idea would be ranked 50.

Step 5. An average ranking for each idea is tabulated.

Step 6. If there is a clear winner, go with that idea. Otherwise, take the top few ideas and try to get the group to agree on one of them.

Discussion Format #3: A Combination: NGT-Storming

Our experience has shown that *NGT-Storming*, a combination of the brainstorming format and the NGT format, is often the best group creativity format.

Step 1: Each individual compiles a list of ideas and questions. Again, the techniques from the previous three chapters should be used at this stage. This can be done before, or at the beginning of, the meeting.

Step 2: A group brainstorming session begins. Group members both contribute entries from their lists and make up new ideas.

Step 3: When the brainstorming session concludes, people should contribute any ideas from their lists that have not yet come up in the discussion.

Step 4: The ideas are discussed.

Step 5: Participants are given some time to consider the ideas on their own. Sometimes it is wise to close the meeting at this stage so that people can go home and "sleep on it."

Step 6: The group tries to reach a consensus about which idea is best. If no consensus can be reached, the ranking system employed in NGT is used to select the "winning" idea.

Discussion Format #4: *Question Questing*

As we have frequently pointed out, the master tool for generating good creative thoughts is a series of good questions. So a particularly effective group discussion format we have developed is *Question Questing*. We recommend that all creative meetings begin with this technique. Question Questing is basically a brainstorming session in which the sole objective is to produce lots of questions. The same rules that apply to group brainstorming apply to Question Questing. All of the techniques for changing the question which we introduced in Chapter 4 should be employed.

At certain times in a Question Questing session, answering a question may be permitted. This applies particularly to informational questions that must be answered before a line of inquiry can be continued. When the leader of the group hears such a question being asked, he or she should say "Answer" and then provide the answer or allow a participant to answer.

Once a lengthy list of questions has been developed, the group should go through the list, question by question, and attempt to provide creative answers.

The following is a sample Question Questing session. (Fred is the leader.):

Fred: Should we build a new conference center?

Jane: Why would we want to build a new conference center?

Liza: Who would we be serving in this conference center?

Will: What work is involved in building it?

Jane: Do conference centers usually make money?

Will: Is there any competition?

Liza: Is the competition making money?

Fred: Answer: There is a conference center 15 miles from here. They broke even last year. What would we do to beat the competition?

Jane: Why do people go to conferences? What do they really want out of a conference center?

Will: Is there a service that our conference center could provide that no one has ever provided before?

Liza: Is there a more appealing name than "conference center?"

Fred: What would happen if we opened up our conference center and then someone else opened a better one?

Will: What does pond scum have to do with conference centers?

Jane: Will we have to increase the water supply to the hotel?

Liza: What about parking?

Fred: In what ways is parking like stacking apples at a grocery store?

Will: Where will we get the money?

Liza: How is the local economy doing?

Will: Is there a local business that would give us some money to start up if we would allow them to hold their conferences in our conference center?

The question quest continues. Eventually there is a lull in the conversation so Fred steps in:

Fred: Let's go through the questioning techniques in Chapter 4 of *INNovation*.

(They go through the chapter ending with . . .)

Liza: . . . Question 14: What color should it be? Question 15: If we had unlimited time and money how would we do it? Question 16: Where will this end?

Fred: OK, any more questions?

Will: Is there a way that we could build it closer to the airport?

Jane: Is there a way we could move the airport closer to the conference center?

Fred: What type of transportation do people prefer to take to an airport?

(The quest continues in this manner until Fred finally says:)

Fred: Who wants to break for coffee?

Jane: What is the meaning of coffee?

Will: What would happen if instead of drinking coffee and smoking tobacco, people smoked coffee and drank tobacco?

(Two hours later . . . :)

Liza: If we build an inside-out, underwater, conference center, what color blimp would we use to transport our customers to the dark room?

When the Question Quest is over, the group would next pursue answers, perhaps by using one of the previous three discussion formats.

The more creative contributions the merrier! It is often the case that creativity is stimulated by other team players, and it is more often the case that less creative people make observations or suggestions that are then incorporated into the final creative idea. The term team player defines a person who works on the what's-right approach and not the who's-right approach.

Charles Feeney
Gerard Atkins & Co. Ltd.

You can motivate others to generate entrepreneurial ideas with praise, encouragement, and financial incentives. Also you should never laugh at or give negative reinforcement for bad ideas.

Charles Mund
President
Service Dynamics Corp.

One final note regarding creative groups: it is important that you inform your employees that they are empowered to be creative. They must be made aware that their input is encouraged and that it will be heard. As employees are given a greater part in the idea-generating and decision-making processes, they become more fluent with their input and more committed to the results. Industry leaders are well aware of this phenomenon.

All employees should be encouraged to take an active role in finding ways to improve the operation. It means letting people have a say in determining the outcome of something that affects them; it means giving people power.

Michael Kay
President
Portman Hotels

In the past, creativity seems to have been a right reserved for management. In the future, enlightened managers will focus on developing creativity in guest-contact employees to improve responsiveness to individual guest's needs. The future of our industry lies in unleashing the tremendous pent-up resources of our non-management employees. We are pushing more authority, responsibility, and accountability to the properties and to lower levels of the organization. I think our next challenge will be to break down barriers and encourage more individual new ideas through creativity in the organization.

> Donald Trice
> President
> Interstate Hotels Corp.

We practice a hands-off management approach and style. We hire people that can be initiators and decision-makers without having to have constant affirmation.

> Carl Winston
> Vice President,
>   Operations
> Motels of America

I want my people to have a piece of the decision. If they have a hand in it, they support it. I never force a decision.

> Andre S. Tatibouet
> President
> Aston Hotels &
>   Resorts

Our number one goal is to get responsibility and authority to the lowest level, our crew.

> Jim Simonson
> Vice President
> Restaurants Unlimited,
>   Inc.

The most difficult obstacle to overcome is to get other people to be creative—to try to get them to act rather than just react. Getting people to break that barrier and start testing their ability to be creative is a challenge.

> Robert Agnello
> President
> Koala Inns

I think the ideal situation is to try to create an environment where creative people can thrive and move into the areas where they can be most productive for the organization.

> Peter Kline
> President
> Harvey Hotels

CHAPTER 6

How to Choose the Right Ideas

In previous chapters we discussed techniques and formats that would help you generate a large number of ideas. We emphasized the notion that you will typically have many bad ideas while generating relatively few good ones. The problem now is to determine which ideas have the greatest potential and which should be discarded.

The process described in this chapter will give you guidance in choosing the one or more ideas that are most acceptable.

THE EASY CASES

Before becoming too analytical, let's consider some easy scenarios that are likely to constitute the majority of cases.

Case 1   You have come up with an idea that is clearly superior to all others generated. It has caught the fancy of both you and your colleagues. Everyone (or at least the vast majority of those involved) agrees that it is the idea to implement. In such a case, don't let your analytical self get in the way of progress—go for it.

Case 2   You face a situation that would permit all good ideas to be tried not just one. If you are attempting to increase breakfast sales, there may be no reason to choose among special prices, specialty items, and guaranteed quick service. You might try them all. If you begin doing a booming breakfast business, you may not be able to determine exactly what the impact of each idea was; however, if your dining room is overflowing in the morning, this will probably be the least of your concerns.

Case 3   You have several good ideas that can be combined to produce a single "best" idea. Perhaps the ideas are good for different reasons. One idea may have revenue-enhancing potential, a second might be good for employee morale, and a third might improve service for the guests. It may be worthwhile exploring whether attributes of each idea could be combined to accomplish all three positive effects. In this case it is not necessary to determine which is the best idea for implementation.

THE SITUATION GETS TOUGHER

The tough case arises when you have generated five or six ideas that seem good, but only one or two can be selected. A clear choice is not evident, combining the ideas is not fruitful, and gut feel does not seem to be a good avenue to pursue.

The selection process consists of three elements:

1. a list of "necessary" selection criteria,
2. a list of "desirable" selection criteria weighted according to their relative importance, and
3. a rating scheme (e.g., a 1–10 scale where 1 is poor and 10 is excellent).

Necessary Selection Criteria

"Necessary" selection criteria, as the name suggests, are criteria that an idea must meet in order to be considered. If the idea fails to satisfy any of the "necessary" criteria, it cannot be considered for implementation, at least not in its present form. For example, the idea

1. must have the potential to increase revenue;
2. must not detract from the current level of guest service;
3. must not adversely affect employee morale;
4. must be in line with the company mission.

The first step, therefore, is to determine which ideas under consideration have fulfilled the "necessary" selection criteria. Second, if an idea fails to meet any of these criteria, you must drop or alter it in such a way as to bring it into line with the "necessary" conditions.

Desirable Selection Criteria

"Desirable" selection criteria are those which will be considered for choosing among the ideas that have survived step one. If the decision involves choosing a new item to include on the menu, the "desirable" criteria might include: sales potential, cost, perceived quality of product, gross profit margin, compatibility with current menu, and availability from competitors. The better the idea satisfies the selection criteria, the better it should be rated for possible implementation.

The "desirable" selection criteria will invariably not carry equal importance. This relative importance of each criterion must be dealt with either explicitly or implicitly. As the decision maker, you may simply recognize that "sales potential" is very important and "availability from competitors" is far less important. On the other hand, you may choose to be considerably more precise in your decision making and attribute specific weights to these selection criteria. For example, the relatively important "sales potential" may carry 30% of the weight in the decision process, while the less important "availability from competitors" may carry only 5% of the weight.

All criteria, important to the final decision, should be included with some reasonable sense of their relative importance specified. This may seem like a very analytical, pedantic, left-brain activity that any self-respecting, right-brain, divergent individual would find objectionable and, therefore, reject. However, we would contend that whether or not you will admit it, you actually carry out such a process any time you make a choice among alternatives. You have some fuzzy bases (dare we say "criteria") in your mind that you realize range (dare we say "have relative importance") from big-time to that-would-be-nice. You then let your mental calculator make the necessary "soft" computations to reach a decision. The process is the same, only the level of formality differs. Therefore, at the risk of having you skip to Chapter 7, allow us to take the slightly more formal approach with this decision process.

The Rating Scheme

The rating scheme is the final element of the decision process. This scheme enables you to rate each idea on each selection criterion. The rating range could be high, medium, and low; it could be excellent, good, fair, and poor; or it might be a 1-to-5 or 1-to-10 scale with the extremes representing least acceptable to most acceptable, respectively. Presumably, the various rating schemes will lead to the same choice if the scales are consistently applied. Terms such as high, low, excellent, and poor may have an appeal to the less quantitative individuals; however, the numeric ratings will force you to be quite exact in the decision process and will enable you to more carefully rank the alternatives. Having come this far with this convergent, left-brain process, let's crank up the calculators and forge ahead. Let's try the ten-point rating scale.

We have now completely defined the three elements to our decision process:

1. The "necessary" criteria have eliminated or caused the alteration of any ideas which violated any of these hurdles. For our illustration, assume five ideas have survived these criteria.
2. The "desirable" criteria have defined the issues to be used to rate and select the ideas. For illustrative purposes, assume five criteria will be used in the selection process. Assume that each of the five criteria has been afforded equal weight. Because the weights must sum to 1 or 100%, each will have a weight of .2 or 20% in the decision process.
3. The rating scale of 1 (low) to 10 (high) will be used to assess how well each idea fits each criterion.

The rating grid might appear as follows:

	Idea 1	Idea 2	Idea 3	Idea 4	Idea 5
Criterion 1 (.2)	8	9	7	8	7
Criterion 2 (.2)	6	8	7	5	9
Criterion 3 (.2)	7	9	6	8	5
Criterion 4 (.2)	5	7	8	9	8
Criterion 5 (.2)	8	6	6	7	9
Weighted average	6.8	7.8	6.8	7.4	7.6

The weighted average for Idea 1 is calculated as follows:

W.A. = (8 × .2) + (6 × .2) + (7 × .2) + (5 × .2) + (8 × .2)
= 1.6 + 1.2 + 1.4 + 1.0 + 1.6 = <u>6.8</u>

The other weighted averages are computed in the same manner. According to these ratings, Idea 2 is the best, followed closely by Idea 5, then Idea 4.

Before selecting the best idea, however, you might ask yourself a couple questions. Is the outcome consistent with what you anticipated? In other words, does it feel right? You might want to reconsider the weights assigned to the five criteria. Is it possible that a small change to these weights would result in a realignment of the ideas? For example, if Criterion 2 or Criterion 5 were weighted more heavily, Idea 5 would likely surpass Idea 2. Are the ratings as they should be? If Idea 4 were not rated quite so poorly on Criterion 2, or if Idea 5 had a bit better rating on Criterion 3, could they both surpass Idea 2?

Be careful, however, of becoming too taken by the apparent exactness of this methodology. Precision is nice but a wrong answer to three decimal places is still a wrong answer. Establishing the criterion weights and estimating the ratings is an inexact process that may give illusions of correctness. If the numbers do not agree with what your feelings tell you is correct, you should re-think the process until you reach a comfort level between what you calculate and what you feel is correct. Your right brain must be comfortable with what your left brain is suggesting.

CHAPTER 7

Blocks to Creativity and How to Smash Them

Creativity can easily be stifled and suffocated when there is no open mindedness and an absence of recognition for change or improvement.

> Michael W. N. Chiu
> President
> Prima Hotels/Holiday Inn

One block to creativity is whether or not management actually uses the creative suggestions to the advantage of the customers, the owners, and the providers of the ideas. Another block can be how creative people are viewed and rewarded and whether they are criticized if a creative idea is unsuccessful. If they are heavily criticized and constantly reminded that it was their idea that didn't work, then they stop being creative.

> J. William Keithan
> Former Senior Vice President
> Westin Hotels and Resorts

In the previous chapters, we discussed the way the creative process is supposed to work. Sometimes, however, the creative process does not work as well as it should. Sometimes the ideas simply don't flow. Sometimes they flow only in certain limited directions.

If ideas are not flowing with complete freedom, you may be experiencing a *block*. A block is anything that prevents you from getting the keys to certain boxes or prevents you from gluing ideas in certain ways. Blocks can be imposed upon you by other people, by the rules and values of your society, or by your own mind.

Blocks must be eliminated so that the ideas can flow freely again. We refer to the tools that are used to eliminate blocks as *sledgehammers*. We refer to the process of eliminating a block as *smashing a block with a sledgehammer*. If you wish to be a creative person and/or a creative manager of other people, you must be vigilant in your search for blocks that may be inhibiting creativity. You must always carry the sledgehammers with which to smash them.

The following lyrics by Harry Chapin provide a poignant example of how blocks inhibit creativity. As you read them, try to think of some of the ways that you, your organization, and your society play the role of the first teacher in the song.

Flowers are Red

The little boy went first day of school
He got some crayons and he started to draw
He put colors all over the paper
For colors was what he saw.
The teacher said, "What are you doing, young man?"
"I'm painting flowers," he said.
She said, "It's not the time for art, young man,
And anyway flowers are green and red.
There's a time for everything , young man
And a way things should be done.
You've got to show concern for everyone else
For you're not the only one."
And she said,
"Flowers are red, young man
And green leaves are green,
There's no need to see flowers any other way
Than the way they always have been seen."

But the little boy said,
"There are so many colors in the rainbow,
So many colors in the morning sun,
So many colors in a flower
And I see every one."

Well the teacher said, "You're sassy
There's ways that things should be,
And you'll paint flowers the way they are

So repeat after me,
'Flowers are red, young man,
And green leaves are green
There's no need to see flowers any other way
Than the way they always have been seen.'"

But the little boy said,
"There are so many colors in the rainbow
So many colors in the morning sun
So many colors in a flower
And I see every one."

The teacher put him in a corner
She said, "It's for your own good.
And you won't come out, till you get it right
And are responding like you should."
Finally he got lonely, frightened thoughts filled his head
So he went up to the teacher and this is what he said,
"Flowers are red,
And green leaves are green,
There's no need to see flowers any other way
Than the way they always have been seen."

Well, time went by like it always does
And they moved to another town,
And the little boy went to another school
And this is what he found,
The teacher there was smiling
She said, "Painting should be fun,
And there are so many colors in the rainbow,
So let's use every one."

But the little boy painted flowers
In neat rows of green and red
And when the teacher asked him why,
This is what he said,

"Flowers are red, and green leaves are green
There's no need to see flowers any other way
Than the way they always have been seen."

© Story Songs Ltd., 1978

SIX BLOCKS AND SIX SLEDGEHAMMERS

Success in the hospitality industry depends upon the ability to "paint a new and better flower" than the competition. There are very few businesses that can afford to coast along painting the same old red and green flowers.

We will discuss the six categories of blocks, and their six corresponding sledgehammers, in terms of ideas presented in the song:[9]

Block 1: "There's no need to see flowers any other way than the way they always have been seen."

In business it is easy to adopt the attitude, "if it ain't broke, don't fix it." Red and green flowers are beautiful, so why change them? This attitude may have its place in some business situations, but it is never good for creativity. It is a block. It stops you from asking questions and considering alternatives. If you are not looking for ways to improve your operation, your operation will not improve.

Ironically, the hospitality organizations that became successful as a result of some highly creative ideas, often begin to suffer from Block 1 as soon as they become successful. This is because they are afraid to attempt risky new projects in which they may lose their prosperity. What such companies fail to realize is that while they are resting on their laurels, other companies not suffering from Block 1 are out there trying to devise ways to put them out of business.

Sledgehammer 1: Look for new and better flowers. Try using some of the many colors in the rainbow, or in the morning sun . . .

The sledgehammer that smashes Block 1 is to adopt the attitude, "Sure it ain't broke, but maybe it could be working even better." If you apply the "How could I change it?" techniques from Chapter 2 to every facet of your organization, you will smash Block 1.

This concept applies not only to products and policies but also to ideas. Never accept an idea because it seems to be "the right idea." Assume that there are always two right ideas and that the one you haven't

---

[9] The categories of mental blocks we have utilized were developed from those presented by James L. Adams in his book *Conceptual Blockbusting*, W. W. Norton & Co., NY, 1979, pp. 13–82.

thought of yet is better than the one you have. Then if you think of a better one, make the assumption again.

Roger von Oech offers a good technique for encouraging people to wield Sledgehammer 1:

> One technique for finding the second right answer is to change the questions you use to probe a problem. For example, how many times have you heard someone say, "What is the answer?" or "What is the meaning of this?" or "What is *the* result?" These people are looking for *the* answer, and *the* meaning, and *the* result. If you train yourself to ask, "What are the answers?" and "What are the meanings?" and "What are the results?" you will find that people will think a little more deeply and offer more than one idea.[10]

> I try to encourage others to try new things. I let them know that if something doesn't work out it is okay as long as they don't try the same non-working idea over and over again. There is no fear of punishment for an idea that doesn't work out.
>
> *Burton Sack*
> *President and CEO*
> *Pub Ventures of New*
> *England, Inc.*

> The key point is to let your people know that you want them to be creative. After they understand the few basics of your business which must not be changed, then you must provide an environment that allows your people to try new things . . . and, to make mistakes! You must also reward their successes. I think the success of whatever they do is the reward for most of the people—the recognition. Financially they can gain from it either through a bonus or other means. Generally, the financial part is not the important issue. If they succeed with their idea, they will get respect and recognition from the people around them.
>
> *Jim Simonson*
> *Vice President*
> *Restaurants Unlimited,*
> *Inc.*

---

[10] Roger von Oech, *A Whack on the Side of the Head: How to Unlock Your Mind for Innovation,* Warner Books, New York, NY, 1983, p. 25.

Block 2: "It's not the time for art, young man, and flowers aren't even my department."

An old hotel story describes a low-level employee returning home with the announcement that he had just been promoted to the position of Vice President in Charge of Coffee. His wife, not believing such a position existed, phoned the hotel to check it out. When she asked the switchboard operator to connect her with the Vice President for Coffee, the operator replied, "Would that be regular or decaffeinated?"

Of course, a Vice President for Decaffeinated Coffee is a bit absurd, but specialization within the hospitality industry is very much a reality. This kind of specialization is sometimes required to carry out the wide range of complex services that guests expect from a hospitality organization; handled incorrectly, however, it can be a block to creativity. An employee, devoted to a limited set of highly specialized activities, is unlikely to open a wide range of boxes or acquire the new boxes that growing and learning offer. Limited boxes result in limited creativity. If all you have are red and green crayons, you will never draw anything but red and green flowers.

Sledgehammer 2: Cross the boundaries into new flower gardens; Borrow other people's crayons.

If the person in charge of buffets does nothing except coordinate buffets, chances are those buffets will not be creative. Suppose, however, that this same person is encouraged

- to watch the way employees are motivated in the housekeeping department,
- to observe how food is prepared so quickly in the snack bar
- to visit other hotels to see how they coordinate their buffets,
- to read about primitive rituals for offering food to the gods.

Then this employee might return with some new ideas and approaches.

Even though an organization may require a high degree of specialization, it should keep open the borders between different departments. It should encourage cross-fertilization of ideas by sometimes inviting an accountant to an interior design meeting or a front desk manager to an F&B meeting.

Indeed, the creative manager of a large resort in the Southeast told us of the time he invited a chef to a marketing meeting. The chef was silent through the first hour of the meeting while the marketers were putting a new vacation package together. Then when they thought they were finished and were about to close the meeting the chef said, "Wait, this package needs a garnish—something extra that will make it special." The marketers took his advice and added celebrity tennis tournaments to the package. Sales doubled.

One leader expressed the importance of having his employees see other organizations.

> The most significant way in which I encourage creativity in the members of our organization is to send key employees overseas to see how other hoteliers run their businesses. For example, I sent two F&B managers to Europe to experience European hospitality. One was a dining room captain and the other was the executive chef of that facility. Since the two must work as a team, I believe that they should also learn as a team. In follow up, I next sent each of their assistants. I also send the chiefs of each major department in the hotel overseas with $10,000. I tell them to make their own travel arrangements, to experience first-hand the customer's point of view—and whether they stay two weeks or two months is up to them.
>
> *Ichiro Inumaru*
> *President & General Manager*
> *Imperial Hotels Ltd.*

> Cross-training of employees among departments can encourage creativity, because the inexperienced new employee views issues from a new point of view. We must find ways to capture these creative ideas before the new employee becomes brainwashed with traditional perspectives.
>
> *Donald Trice*
> *President*
> *Interstate Hotels Corp.*

> I do cross-pollination with employees. People placed temporarily in different environments are more creative than if they are in the same situation day after day. By moving employees among different locations,

I help them to generate new ideas. I also solicit ideas from employees at all levels.

> Burton Sack
> President and CEO
> Pub Ventures of New
> England, Inc.

Moving people from their normal environment is helpful in enhancing their creativity.

> Richard Ferris
> Former President
> United Airlines

Block 3: "I can only paint flowers in neat rows of red and green; I don't know how to use all the colors in the rainbow."

Block 3 is a lack of confidence in your creative abilities. If you think you do not have the ability to think creative thoughts, then you will not think creative thoughts. If you do not approach the world with an attitude that says, "I am going to have a great idea today," then you will not look for great ideas. If you don't look for great ideas, you will not find them.

Sledgehammer 3: Force yourself to use every crayon in the box.

Recognize that scientists have yet to discover, and probably never will discover, a gene that determines how creative a person will be. If a person is extremely creative, it is probably because that person has developed certain thinking habits that lead to creative ideas. He or she automatically uses many of the creativity techniques discussed in the earlier chapters of this book. If a person seems to be extremely *uncreative* it is probably because he or she has none of these habits, never questions anything, and never considers new ways of doing things. In neither case does the person's creativity level result from some inborn trait.

If creativity derives from mental habits rather than innate abilities, then becoming more creative is simply a matter of acquiring the right mental habits. You can learn to question everything; you can start applying the creativity techniques to your daily life. Take a problem and force yourself to think of 101 ideas about how to solve it.

We have never found an exception to this statement: You cannot help but be creative if you just take the time to try.

I think I've learned to encourage people to do things. What stifles creativity is to be hyper-critical of somebody to point out the things they do wrong all the time. That doesn't do much for creativity. You must encourage people to do things and don't worry if it doesn't work, just try again. You are not a bad person because it didn't work; you are a good person because you tried it. It is important to create an atmosphere that allows people to try things, to fail or to succeed, and not to be criticized for it. That is what develops creativity.

> Donald Berens
> Owner
> D. P. Berens Inc.
> Specialty Services

Block 4: "Painting should not be fun."

Some people take themselves and their jobs too seriously. When people start joking at a meeting they might say, "Let's get serious." When a discussion wanders off topic they might say, "Let's get back to business."

But what is humor? Humor is looking at things in unusual ways, tampering with accepted ways of doing things, disregarding accepted values. As you probably noticed, the definition of humor sounds a lot like the definition of creativity.

There is a logical basis to the suggestion that humor and creativity naturally go together. The fear of failing, or of being wrong, foolish, or different can stifle creativity. Humor, however, encourages us to be foolish and to see things differently. In fact, when it comes to being humorous, the more foolish we are, the more successful we become. So the first benefit of humor is that it temporarily puts on hold the fears that inhibit our creativity.

In addition, humor itself is often quite creative. Humor often results from our connecting two concepts in a different and hopefully funny manner. The result is that you see the issue in a different way. We find it funny when a comedian such as Steven Wright tells us that he accidentally inserted his ignition key in his apartment door; when he turned it the apartment started up, and he decided to drive it around for a while. Likewise, we are amused when he tells us that he mistakenly tried to turn his television on with his garage door opener; the TV screen rolled up exposing a tiny rake and lawn mower inside. Mixing the functions of car and apartment keys or garage door openers and TV remote control units is the type of creative connection which we are seeking. Seeing items in a different way is the essence of creativity. The second benefit of humor, therefore, is to activate your mind to think in a creative way.

Finally, when humor is applied to a problem or opportunity in your business, it helps you to see the situation in a different way. Direct your humor toward the salad bar, the check-in counter, the under-used restaurant, or the over-booked rooms, and see what this humorous look might suggest. While the humor may not provide you with a direct solution, it will certainly get you thinking about the situation from a different angle, and that is the first step in reaching a creative solution.

Too often the environment in an organization is too somber and is not conducive to humor. When people feel that they must always be serious, they tend to limit their thoughts. They don't allow their minds to wander. This is a block to creativity.

Sledgehammer 4: Painting should be fun!

Smashing Block 4 is simple and fun—all you have to do is learn to enjoy yourself. But joking and playing are useful as more than just an ice-breaker. They actually lead to good ideas. For example

> Silliness is important in coming up with creative ideas. I take great pride in acting like I am twelve years old. I can see many different things from the perspective of a twelve-year-old that will benefit my customers.
>
> *Stan Bromley*
> *Regional Vice President/General Manager*
> *Four Seasons Hotel Washington*

> I put on different wild and crazy parties for the staff. The Suppressed Desire Day party helps to loosen people up and invigorate them. At this party I give out $100 to the individual with the best costume. We also have skits and other mechanisms for bringing about a closeness and looseness that permits people to do their best at coming up with creative ideas.
>
> *Trisha Wilson*
> *President*
> *Wilson & Associates*

Closely related to having fun is having a good sense of humor, which is perceived by many of our innovative industry leaders as being essential to the creative process.

> Without a sense of humor you cannot be creative.
> Chris Hemmeter
> Senior Partner
> Hemmeter Investment
> Co.

> A sense of humor is important in the creative process, because it helps get the ball rolling. Humor changes the stride so that you can attack the problem in a new way or see it from a new angle.
> William V. Eaton
> Senior Principal
> Cini-Little
> International

> A good sense of humor plays a crucial role in that it acts as a catalyst in bringing the ideas together in new ways.
> Leslie W. Stern
> President
> L. W. Stern
> Associates, Inc.

> To be creative you have to have a good sense of humor.
> William Callnin
> President
> Atlantic Inns
> Management, Inc.

Block 5: "There's a way things should be done." (Follow rules.)

People like to make rules. Rules make life simpler. One of the ways rules do this is by keeping us from having to think. For example, most people do not decide for themselves whether or not to grow grass around their homes. It is just expected they will. However, they could instead think about the pros and cons, make a decision, and then be prepared to back-up that decision. Some people have come up with creative alternatives, such as rocks, polished stones, sand, slate, artificial turf, or wood chips. These alternatives would not need to be watered, mowed, edged, or chemically treated. But most people do not bother to think about it—the convention of lawns has obviated the need to think. A lawn may be a good convention, but like all rules or conventions, it is a block to creativity.

Rules seem to be essential to the smooth functioning of families, businesses, schools, and societies. We have written rules and unwritten rules. We have rules that we follow without even knowing why we follow them. For example, you almost never stand with your back to a person to whom you are speaking. You are unwittingly following a rule that says, "Thou shalt face the person with whom thou art speaking."

Creativity depends upon breaking rules, doing something in a way that no one has done it before. Whenever you follow rules, you are doing things the way everyone has done them before. The history of creative thought is a history of breaking rules. Copernicus broke the rule that the sun revolved around the earth when he advanced his theory of how the solar system really worked. Architect Isaiah Rogers broke with centuries of inn tradition in 1828 by building Boston's Tremont House, the world's first "modern" hotel. In this century, Portman (designer of "atrium" hotels) continued to revolutionize the physical shape of hotels, while Bill Marriott proved that a luxury hotel *could* be built in a rundown neighborhood like Times Square when he built the New York Marriott Marquis.

An organization that promotes the mentality that the rules must always be followed in suffering from a creative block.

Sledgehammer 5: Ask: "Why are flowers red and leaves green?" Create an organizational climate in which people are encouraged to break rules for creative purposes.

This is a two-part sledgehammer. The first part is always to question the rules. Ask, "Who says the sun revolves around the earth?" "Why is the front desk procedure this way?" "Why is there an unwritten rule that discourages us from singing during staff meetings?" Ask, "Why are the keys on a computer keyboard in that order?"[11] As long as you question the rules, they will never hamper your creativity.

Sometimes you will come to the conclusion that the rules are good

---

[11] It is not because that pattern is the most efficient. In fact, it is because that pattern is the least efficient. It was designed in the days of the manual typewriter in order to slow typists down so that the keys would not stick.

rules and that thinking about them will simply increase your understanding of them. Sometimes you will come to the conclusion that they are bad rules and that thinking about them will lead to creative improvement or innovation. Recognize that many people are averse to questioning and changing things. If you are always questioning things, you will probably have to endure the disapproval of uncreative people; but the rewards of being a free-thinking creative person will make it worthwhile.

The second part of this sledgehammer is to promote an organization in which the rules are flexible. Let people know that they are free to break or bend the rules as long as it is for creative purposes.

> I expect my employees to act like adults by thinking and using their heads. No one will ever be punished around here for making what they consider to be a good decision. I believe in psychic rewards as well as monetary rewards. In other words, if someone has a good idea, their reward might be my taking their memo and writing "spectacular idea—let's get started on it next week!" If this memo is circulated to half a dozen other people, then they all know that this person came up with a spectacular idea. By getting credit for the idea, the person is praised or, in other words, rewarded.
>
> *John Alexander*
> *President*
> *The CBORD Group*
> *Inc.*

Block 6: "But what if I make a black flower and no one likes it? What if it dies?"

A lot of people are afraid of their creative ideas. They think, "There must be a good reason why no one has ever tried it this way," or "What if I fail?" The fear of failure is a serious block to creativity. It is also a deeply ingrained block. From the earliest days of our schooling we are taught that there are right answers and wrong answers, and we are punished for offering the wrong answer.

People who are afraid of failing will not only be afraid to implement their creative ideas, but they will also tend to follow the thinking rules that have been used successfully in the past rather than trying to devise their own creative rules; therefore they will have fewer creative ideas.

Sledgehammer 6:   Realize the benefits of failure.

Thomas J. Watson, the founder of IBM, once said, "The way to succeed is to double your failure rate."

Carl Winston said, "If I'm not failing at least 25 percent of the time then I'm not being adventurous enough in my thinking."

What these creative people are confirming is that failure is an essential part of the creative process. Creative ideas are often risky ideas. When you implement an idea that no one has ever implemented before, you are blazing new trails and there is no guide to keep you from getting lost. Creative people are willing to take these risks. Edison was willing to fail 749 times before he found the right filament for his light bulb.

Another benefit of failure is that it often leads to new ideas that are successful. Columbus, after all, had been trying to sail to India. Popcorn was invented when Indian corn fields accidentally caught fire. Charles Goodyear discovered how to vulcanize rubber when he accidentally dropped a mixture of rubber, white lead, and sulphur onto a hot stove. Failure in one endeavor often leads directly or indirectly to success in another.

> No one has ever been fired from our organization for making a mistake. If they make the same mistake repeatedly, that is a problem. But if they learn from their mistakes, and we ask the right questions about why it happened, why it didn't work, and people don't get too intimidated by that, then we can accept the mistake. They have to be prepared to accept the questioning of why it didn't work without necessarily being reprimanded for trying it. Well-motivated mistakes are good investments. The biggest reward system that most creative people are looking for in my experience is the ability to continue to be creative. That's a bigger reward than the specific cash equity that comes out of it. That kind of reward system is in place in our organization. People who have good ideas are allowed to develop them, and we try to find situations where they can make contributions.
>
> Peter Kline
> President
> Harvey Hotels

I remember one of my bosses saying, "Now don't forget, you get paid to make mistakes too, just don't make the same one too many times." What he was saying is we will take some chances and try things, and if you're not right, that's all right; at least you're not going to be sitting there doing the same thing the same way forever. I think those are the kinds of things that get people excited, and it pays to have people try new things; that's what creativity is all about. I think the way you encourage creativity is you try to create an environment where people feel very comfortable about speaking up and suggesting things. I never really put someone down or make the comment, "that's a stupid idea"; we don't need those kinds of responses. I think you can always foster a feeling that it is perfectly all right. You can make a statement about a good idea; and there are ways to say that maybe it isn't so good without anyone getting too annoyed.

> Fred Eydt
> President
> The Watermark
> Group, Inc.

Failing is a risk that creative people continually face. It is not comfortable, but it is necessary to the innovative process. Without some risk, there cannot be creativity.

In order to make an event special, you have to take risks.

> Jane B. Tatibouet
> Vice President,
> Human Resources
> Aston Hotels &
> Resorts

If you are not willing to take risks, you may never know or realize your full potential. Furthermore, your "happiness quotient" for success will diminish due to the suppression of your creative energies.

> Thomas M. Gneiting
> Manager—Corporate
> Services
> Federal Express Corp.

I search out weird things. I try things that haven't been tried before. I need to be a pace setter. I like my hotel company to be first in thinking up new guest pleasers.

> Stan Bromley
> Regional Vice
> President/General
> Manager
> Four Seasons Hotel
> Washington

I have a need and a desire to be a risk taker.

Michael Kay
President
Portman Hotels

The "INNovation" philosophy should be looked at this way:
1. You think up 101 ideas.
2. You select a few good ones.
3. You try one of them.
4. If it fails, you learn from your mistake.
5. You try another idea.

CHAPTER 8

Selling Your Ideas

> Being able to see the big picture is very important to being creative. It helps you know your means and your extremes. It gives you flexibility to confront barriers when you are trying to get approval for an idea.
>
> James Rouse
> The Enterprise
> Foundation

Understanding the creative unblocking tools (Chapter 7) along with the nineteen techniques for generating new and creative ideas (Chapters 2–4), puts you well on your way through the creative process. However, you need to take another important step to complete the process: presenting and selling your creative idea to others.

Countless books and articles have been written describing various technological and scientific ideas that revolutionized an industry or made the inventor a fortune. However, the majority of those publications fail to address the fact that those "famous" ideas did not sell themselves. Behind every famous creative idea is a person or group of people who have worked to sell that idea to others. This is not to say that there will always be a monumental struggle involved in the selling process. Some ideas are easier to sell than others. However, whether an idea requires a little or a great deal of selling effort, it still takes a game plan, or selling framework, to structure that effort in a productive manner. Many people find developing the selling strategy and then presenting the idea to be the hardest part of the creative process. Yet this should not be the case, and will not be if you subscribe to the following guidelines:

1. When creating your selling plan you should:
   a. really know your idea

    b. determine who is going to "buy" your idea and develop a selling plan based on the buyer's needs
    c. understand your buyer's communication style
2. When making the presentation you should:
    a. present your idea in a timely fashion
    b. establish a relationship of trust between yourself and the prospect
    c. be creative

REALLY KNOW YOUR IDEA

First, before you begin to think about selling your creative idea to someone, sleep on it. Get to know your idea inside and out, play with it, challenge it, nurture it. Figure out all of its features or attributes, the negative ones as well as the positive ones, and try to put in concrete terms why you think your idea is a winner.

In Chapter 6, "How to Choose the Right Ideas," you were shown how to winnow the good ideas from the rest of the pack. You compare the idea's strengths and weaknesses and see how each measures up to the others in terms of implementation costs and benefits, long-term vs. short-term use, etc. As you are mulling over the idea, you should do the same strengths-vs.-weaknesses analysis on the attributes of your idea. What are its positive and negative attributes? In other words, why would someone buy or reject your idea? What problem(s) would it solve or what benefit(s) would it create for the buyer? Then, as you begin to develop your selling strategy, you can work on ways to accent the positive features of your idea, playing down the negative attributes, and you will be prepared if and when the buyer raises objections to the idea.

After you have really picked apart the idea in your head, talk with a friend, spouse, or colleague who will listen and can offer constructive, objective feedback. Ask any of them to play devil's advocate and come up with reasons why the idea will not work. You will be amazed at the helpful feedback you will receive by asking people who are not directly involved in the situation in which the idea will be used. Finally, after you have batted the idea around, try to figure out what ramifications or consequences your idea will create if accepted. For example, if your idea is one that will cause the layoff of many of your co-workers and friends, even though it would give you a promotion, you may think twice about selling that idea without contingency plans developed to aid those whose jobs would be jeopardized.

DETERMINE YOUR BUYER AND YOUR BUYER'S NEEDS

The next step is to determine who will be most receptive to your idea and will help you get your idea off the ground and working. Are you going to sell your idea to your boss, your co-workers or peers, your customers or clients, your subordinates? The major factor in your choice is who is in the position to understand and capitalize on the benefits of your idea. This means that you must present your idea to the person who has the power to make a "yes" decision. Usually, the higher up in the organization the "yes" person is, the better.

Once you have settled on the "target buyer" of your idea, start thinking in terms of the buyer's needs and wants. The first stage in your selling plan should be to develop a framework that caters to the buyer's needs. Look at your idea from the buyer's viewpoint. For example, why will your boss want to buy into your idea? Try to get inside his or her head and draw conclusions about your idea, based on how you think the buyer will react to it. In this way, and only in this way, can you develop a successful game plan to sell your idea.

In economic bottom-line terms, idea selling translates into determining how the idea affects the buyer's "personal utility." By personal utility, we mean the type of personal advantages the buyer will receive if he or she accepts your idea. If the idea works, will the buyer receive a raise, a promotion, a feeling of accomplishment, and so on? Most people buy into ideas in order to maximize their personal utility in a personal situation or setting. Therefore, pick the buyer whose personal utility will be enhanced the most if the idea works.

When you are developing your selling strategy, make sure you are working toward an outcome that is balanced. The perceived benefits for both the buyer and you should be equal. Upon accepting your creative idea, the buyer should feel like a winner, and you should feel like a winner for having sold it. In the short run you may be able to sell your idea on promises, smooth talk, or political maneuvering. However, if the idea itself provides no lasting benefit, the buyer will feel cheated.

Therefore, as you plan your selling strategy, make sure that a loser-winner relationship does not develop between you and the buyer.

KNOW YOUR BUYER'S COMMUNICATION STYLE

Before you make your presentation, you need to know the communication style of the prospective buyer. We have found that the best way to structure your presentation is to observe how the buyer communicates and then adapt your presentation to the buyer's communication style.

Part of analyzing the buyer's needs involves understanding the buyer's nonverbal behaviors. Research has shown that within any organization, nonverbal communication highly influences both the way managers make decisions and how they create, shape, and maintain relationships with their fellow employees.[12] Numerous studies also have revealed that people are more strongly influenced by nonverbal cues accompanying a verbal message than by the words actually spoken. In one particular study,[13] it was shown that the overall meaning derived from a verbal message is conveyed 93 percent by nonverbal cues and only 7 percent by the words.

Therefore, learn to read a person's nonverbal as well as verbal signals. These signals can help you to manage your relationship better in terms of what the buyer wants. For example, if the person to whom you are trying to sell your idea does not waste words and is only interested in the bottom line, then your presentation should not contain time-wasting glitz and anecdotes. However, if your prospective buyer demonstrates relaxed social mannerisms, such as loosening his tie and leaning back in his chair, he may be communicating to you that a hard-hitting bottom-line selling approach may not be appropriate in your presentation.

Only by adapting your communication style to fit the buyer's can you package your ideas in a way that can be easily understood and accepted by the buyer! Remember, just having the idea is not good enough. Only when you fully understand both parts of the equation

---

[12] Dalmar Fisher, *Communication In Organizations*, West Publishing Co., St. Paul, MN, 1981, pp. 117–139.

[13] Albert Mehrabian, *Silent Messages*, Wadsworth Publishing Co., Belmont, CA, 1971, pp. 42–47.

(knowing your idea + knowing the buyer = framework for a successful presentation) can you begin to work on developing your presentation.

WATCH YOUR TIMING

Timing is a critical factor to take into consideration as you organize your presentation. Because your opening encounter with the buyer always has a major impact on the success of your presentation and your ability to make the sale, it is most important that the odds of success are stacked in your favor. If you know that your boss is grumpy in the morning, make an appointment for the afternoon. Also remember to evaluate the timing of your presentation with the various business and working cycles of your buyer's company. For example, if on the one hand you are presenting a new capital-intensive idea to a board of directors who just learned that the company's annual profits had declined by fifty percent, it is likely that the outcome of the presentation will not be favorable. On the other hand, if you are presenting to a group of managers who just received large bonuses, they may be thinking in terms of how your idea could help them receive even bigger bonuses next year. Therefore, use timing to your advantage.

ESTABLISH A RELATIONSHIP OF TRUST

Consumer behavior researchers analyze the concept of perceived risk on the part of the buyer. They discuss the buyer's concern that, once he has made the decision to buy an idea or product, he must live with the consequences. It is therefore incumbent upon the seller to minimize the buyer's perceived risk by getting into the decision-making process with the buyer as early as possible. By doing this, you share the decision making and develop a sense on the part of the buyer that you share the perceived risk. Therefore, building trust with the buyer means building a relationship that focuses on helping the buyer make the right decision while minimizing perceived risk.

To nurture the relationship, try to make your buyer feel as comfortable as possible. First, it is important to give your buyer a big broad smile, not just with your mouth but with your whole body. A seller who is truly happy with the opportunity to present an idea will be able to express that happiness in the way he or she communicates with the prospective buyer. Because genuine enthusiasm is contagious, you will find that your state of happiness will positively affect the buyer's mood.

Another way of establishing trust is to describe your idea, using terms that will appeal to the buyer. For example, if you know that your buyer is a big tennis fan, talk in terms of aces and match points. In addition, research has shown that, when a person actively processes and thinks about an idea, it stays with him longer and has a bigger impact. Therefore you want your buyer to think actively about your idea in terms with which he or she is comfortable, so it will be easier for the buyer to understand and evaluate what you are selling. Many buyers immediately become suspicious of a salesperson who uses words and phrases that are unfamiliar.

Finally, if you are able to pre-test your idea, by all means do so. People tend to trust ideas that have shown some type of success, even if that success plays only a small role in the overall idea.

BE CREATIVE

To get the buyer in a receptive mood, try to develop a creative selling strategy. Being creative does not mean relying on multi-media presentation devices to sell your idea. What it does mean is presenting your idea in a new form or new way that provokes buyer interest. For example, a woman we know was not having success in her job interviews. She had strong qualifications but never received any offers. Finally, after several unsuccessful interviews, she came up with the following creative selling idea: she laminated her resume onto a folder. How did this creative idea help her?

First, because the resume was presented in a new form, the interviewers immediately took notice and commented on the uniqueness of her design. Second, because the resume was actually a usable folder, the interviewers tended to use it to store other applicants' resumes. When the interviewer reviewed the resumes, guess which one the interviewer always saw first?

Finally, before you start putting together the actual presentation, determine the likelihood of being 100 percent successful in selling the idea. Total success often is reached incrementally. More "yeses" along the way will decrease the chance of getting a "no" to the overall request.

Plan your selling strategy carefully and be prepared to answer questions regarding all attributes of the idea in a manner that is both creative and thought-provoking.

MAKING THE PRESENTATION

When the time comes to present your idea, your concern should be communication. Communications, whether written, verbal, or nonverbal, is a difficult skill to perfect. Some managers like to think of communication as an art to be perfected through the development of various styles and techniques. When you make your presentation, you should think of the communication process as a work of art in progress with four distinct components: the words you speak, the words you write, the words you convey through body language, and the words you hear. Each component is like an artist's brush or sculptor's chisel, creating the medium through which you can sell your creative idea. Just as the artist understands the difference between chiaroscuro and depth, you should understand how the four components of communication work together to produce an effective presentation. In the following section we will discuss how you should use the four components of communication to create a successful presentation.

The Words You Speak

The first thing you should do when making your presentation is to replace the "I" mentality with the "you" mentality. People who come to selling presentations are concerned with themselves and with how your idea will help them. Therefore, when you are talking, never use lines like "I feel comfortable with this idea . . . " or "I get excited when I think about . . . " Replacing "I" with "you" conveys to the buyer that you are thinking in terms of his or her interests.

Next, organize your presentation into coherent sections: attention getter, introduction, body, and conclusion. The old saying, "Tell them what you are going to say, say it, and tell them what you said" still holds true and for good reason. You want to make sure the buyer clearly follows what you are saying. Keep your presentation as simple as possible. Don't include a lot of buzz words or incomprehensible phrases. Remember, the best ideas are the simplest ideas.

Do not memorize your presentation. Use an outline or note cards which list the main points you want to cover during your presentation. If you memorize, you will not be able to interact with the buyer during your presentation. In addition, the memorization process tends to zap enthusiasm and spontaneity, two important communication attributes that are essential for a successful presentation. Enthusiasm is important because it bolsters your own courage and it is contagious. Spontaneity is essential because it keeps your presentation flexible and allows you to adapt to external occurrences that may not have been foreseen when you planned the presentation.

Finally, make your audience participate in the presentation. Ask them questions or provide them with the opportunity to ask you questions during the presentation. Audience interaction helps establish a relationship in the mind of the participant between a memorable event and your idea.

The Words You Write

Use visual aids such as posters or overheads to help guide your audience through your presentation. A person's attention span is short; you can count on losing your listener's attention at least once during the presentation. Therefore you need to have a visual aid which will get the listener back on track after a "phase-out" has occurred. In addition, each visual aid should address only one or two distinct concepts or thoughts at a time. To get the most out of a visual aid, first get the buyer interested in what you are saying, then hit him with a visual. This approach helps the buyer remember the key verbal statements because they have been reinforced by visual impacts. Finally, keep your visual practical. You do not want to confuse your prospective buyer with a lot of distractions and visual overload. Visual aids should only reinforce the main concepts of your presentation.

The Words Your Body Speaks

Get a good night's sleep. You want to be in a relaxed and wakeful state when presenting your idea. If you look like you just pulled ten sleepless nights in a row, the people to whom you are presenting will be more concerned with calling a doctor for you than listening to your idea.

Furthermore you must practice, practice, practice your presentation. Only when you know your presentation well can your body relax and be its natural self. Also, be aware of your image or "stage presence." Practice in front of a mirror so you can evaluate your appearance and posture. How you look and how you communicate is just as important as what you are saying. Therefore, dress the part you are trying to play. Do not let your appearance compete with your idea.

The Words You Hear

Just as important as how you speak during your presentation is how you listen. Your presentation may go off without a hitch, but if you seem uninterested during the question-and-answer period, you will lose the buyer's trust. When you are giving a presentation, make sure that you are not so wrapped up in what you are saying that you cannot actively listen to comments from the buyer. What we mean by active listening is not just nodding your head in agreement. You must show through your body language and your ability to empathize that you are truly concerned with the buyer's comments or objections and that you can put yourself in his or her shoes. Too often the seller falls into a "fake" listening mode. Then, when the buyer asks for a response, the seller has to reply, "What did you say?" In addition, do not think of objections or critical comments as emotions but as logical thoughts that can be dealt with in a logical manner. Enthusiastically responding to objections to your idea and trying to solve them in terms of the buyer's needs show the buyer that you are on his or her side and that you are both trying to make the idea work.

BE PATIENT AND PERSISTENT

Patience and persistence are two key ingredients in the selling process. Be patient! Just as there are 100 bad ideas for each good one, it might take you 100 selling prospects until you locate the right person to buy into your idea. And, be persistent. People cannot read minds. If you do not tell them about your idea, nobody will. If you think you have a creative idea, go with it and stick with it.

CHAPTER 9

After Words

We conducted extensive interviews with more than fifty hospitality industry leaders who were deemed creative by their peers. Much of the wisdom of these individuals has been included in the preceding chapters; however, additional valuable insights about issues not discussed specifically in the text were brought to our attention by these industry leaders. In this chapter, we will share these additional thoughts.

The first section includes two important issues in the creative process: Creativity as a Full-Time Business and Rewarding Creativity. The second section contains descriptions of the characteristics which the industry leaders believe creative individuals possess: Self Confidence, Patience to Enable Incubation, High Energy Levels, and Desire to Learn. The third section details the characteristics that the industry leaders look for in their own employees.

CREATIVE INDUSTRY LEADERS FOCUS ON ISSUES IMPORTANT TO THE CREATIVE PROCESS

Creativity as a Full-Time Business

> I spend almost all of my waking hours thinking about new and better ways of doing things.
>
> Jane B. Tatibouet
> Vice President,
>   Human Resources
> Aston Hotels &
>   Resorts

Setting aside time for creative thinking is nonsense—you think all the time and hopefully out of all the ideas comes a good one.

Michael Leven
President
Days Inns

When you care about a problem, you keep thinking about it all the time.

Chiaki Tanuma
Executive Vice
President
Green House Co.,
Ltd.

I am constantly looking at everything that surrounds me and thinking about designs and projects.

Keith Talbert
Founder/President
Urban West

Rewarding Creativity

If an organization wants creativity, it has to develop an atmosphere where people are rewarded just for trying.

Donald Strang
President
Strang Corporation

Letting people know by telling them that they did a good job is one of the best ways to keep producing results.

James Rouse
The Enterprise
Foundation

The reward is the application of the idea.

Michael Leven
President
Days Inns

The reward is recognition: private and public acknowledgement of accomplishment; recognition of talent and contribution.

> G. Michael Hostage
> Owner
> G. M. Hostage, Inc.

Sometimes the rewards are financial.

We have contests at individual properties; whichever hotel has the best idea wins several hundred to a few thousand dollars to have a party. The financial benefit far exceeds the cost of the reward.

> Roger Dow
> Vice President, Sales
> & Marketing
> Services
> Marriott Hotels and
> Resorts

To encourage creativity, I offer an all-expense-paid vacation to the team that has the best presentation.

> Stephen Rushmore
> President
> Hospitality Valuation
> Services

Our "Bright Lights Program" pays employees $500 as a reward for their creative ideas.

> Linda Schwabe
> Creative Gourmets

To recognize those who contribute creativity and produce results, part ownership and shared profits are essential elements in insuring continual fertilization of the minds.

> Michael W. N. Chiu
> President
> Prima Hotels/Holiday
> Inn

CHARACTERISTICS THAT CREATIVE INDUSTRY LEADERS EMPHASIZE

Our creative industry leaders emphasize four vital characteristics that they consider significant for their creativity.

Self-Confidence

Self-confidence is an important part of creative leadership. You need confidence in your vision and decision making.

> Andre S. Tatibouet
> President
> Aston Hotels &
>   Resorts

Self esteem is a very important part of being creative. It allows you to be different and not conform to the way things have always been done.

> Chris Hemmeter
> Senior Partner
> Hemmeter Investment
>   Co.

Experience and wisdom help, but I think a lot of creativity has to do with confidence.

> Robert Agnello
> President
> Koala Inns

Patience to Enable Incubation

I find when I have a problem, I must move away from it for a while. I guess it goes into the subconscious and stays there. At any time the ideas might come out.

> G. Michael Hostage
> Owner
> G. M. Hostage, Inc.

I think ideas come to me mostly when I am not thinking about it. After I have worked with a problem and it is going around in the back of my head, all of a sudden there is the idea. Maybe it is a relaxing moment rather than when I am under a great deal of pressure.

>Richard Ferris
>Former President
>United Airlines

High Energy

I'm supercharged. I am running scared all the time. I am constantly wondering about who is going to be us if we are not us.

>Stan Bromley
>Regional Vice President/General Manager
>Four Seasons Hotel
>Washington

The high level of energy, the high level of integrity, the striving for excellence, the desire to be in charge—those traits feed on us all the time.

>Linda Schwabe
>Creative Gourmets

Desire To Learn

You have to have an attitude about yourself in which you never stop learning and growing.

>J. Willard Marriott, Jr.
>President
>Marriott Corporation

I am like a student—always learning new things. I am always considering new thoughts and listening to people's message behind the words.

>Michael Kay
>President
>Portman Hotels

Creativity demands a combination of experience and remaining current with the world.

Henri Lewin
Chairman and CEO
Aristocrat Hotels, Inc.

I go to many seminars, some of which stimulate my thinking. Many of my ideas developed as a result of my attendance at these seminars. I am always committed to learning and growing.

Shoji Yonehama
President
Ringer Hut U.S.A.
Corporation

Creativity is both creating something and being sensitive to what's going on in the world around you. This is essential for making evolutionary changes in your business. You need to experience what is going on in the world to be creative.

Donald Strang
President
Strang Corporation

To be creative, I have to be involved with what is happening today, be that on an informal or formal level—read the papers, go to current movies and plays. I have to ask myself, "What is society asking for? What do people want?"

Hans Bremstrom
President
Sara Hotels
Management
Corp.

DESIRED CHARACTERISTICS OF EMPLOYEES

Creative industry leaders described characteristics they desired in their employees.

I look for active, involved people who are not afraid to speak their minds. I look for people with a track record of being doers.

> Roger Dow
> Vice President, Sales
> & Marketing
> Services
> Marriott Hotels and
> Resorts

Normally I like people who have the courage to try something that is not permissible, who also have enough confidence to think they can make it work.

> Peter Kline
> President
> Harvey Hotels

I try to find people with a diversity of backgrounds.

> John Alexander
> President
> The CBORD Group
> Inc.

I like to have employees who are young, aggressive, articulate, energetic, usually less experienced in the position than they should be.

> Robert Colombo
> General Manager
> Grand Hyatt Hotel
> New York

What I look for in my employees are attitude and individuality.

> Trisha Wilson
> President
> Wilson & Associates

It is important for us to have a wide diversity of employees whom we feel are the main contributors to our company's creativity.

> Linda Schwabe
> Creative Gourmets

CONCLUSION

We began this book with a series of statements from people in the hospitality industry who felt that their ability to be creative has improved the quality of their lives. They have found innovation to be a source of enjoyment, satisfaction, and success. We close this book with the hope that our attempt to enhance your creative abilities has given you tools that will lead you to more enjoyment, satisfaction, and success.

Index

A

Action Rules	53–54
Adapt	25
Agnello, Robert	14, 68, 104
Albrecht, Karl	41
Alexander, John	14, 87, 107
Athanas, Anthony	35
Attribute Listing	22–24, 26, 62

B

Barger, Richard	10, 30
Baum, Joseph H.	15
Berens, Donald	11, 59, 83
Blocks	75–89
Bradley, Richard	2, 8, 34
Brainstorming	60–62
Bremstrom, Hans B.	42, 106
Broader Questions	47–48
Bromley, Stan	2, 84, 89, 105
Burns, Robert	2
Buyers	93–95
Needs	93–94
Communication Styles	94–95

C

Callnin, William J.	85
Chapin, Harry	76
Characteristics, Personal	104–106
Desire to Learn	105–106
Energy	105
Patients	104–105
Self Confidence	104
Chiu, Michael W. N.	3, 4, 75, 103
Colombo, Robert P.	45, 107
Columbus	88
Combine	25
Consequence Questions	50
Copernicus	86
Cross-Training	81–82

D

D'Arienzo, Carmel	40
Definition	4–5, 7–9
Desirable Criteria	71
Desire to Learn	105–106
Design Tree	27–29, 62
Dow, Roger	16, 103, 107
Drucker, Peter	39

E

Eaton, William V.	4, 35, 85
Eberhardt, William	4, 30
Eberle, Robert	25
Edison, Thomas	7, 88
Energy	105
Einstein, Albert	11
Eliminate	25, 26
Eydt, Fred	14, 89

F

Fear of Failure	87–89
Feeney, Charles	10, 39, 67
Ferris, Richard J.	59, 82, 105
Fisher, Dalmar	94
"Flowers Are Red"	76–77
Follow the Rules	85–87
Free Association	15–17, 35, 62
Freud, Sigmund	9
Full-Time Business	101–102

G

Glue	9, 11, 12, 18, 36, 55, 75
Gneiting, Thomas M.	89
Goldstein, Joyce	24
Goodyear, Charles	88

H

Hanson, Bjorn R. L.	47–48
Hemmeter, Chris	1, 8, 42, 85, 104
Hostage, G. Michael	35, 103, 104
Humor	83–85

I

Incubation	104–105
Innovative Imitation	39
Inside-Out Questions	49
Inumaru, Ichiro	13, 81

K

Kay, Michael	11, 58, 67, 90, 105
Keithan, J. William	58, 75
Keys	9, 10, 11, 12, 18, 34, 49
Kline, Peter	10, 35, 68, 88, 107
Kroc, Ray	22

L

Leven, Michael	1, 33, 43, 57, 102(2)
Lewin, Henri	106
List of Questions	52–54
Listening	99
Lists	35–36

M

Magnify	25
Mariani, John	58
Marriott, J. Willard Jr.	7, 42, 50, 57, 86, 105
Marriott Marquis	86
Matrix Analysis	28, 62
Mehrabian, Albert	94
Merle, H. Etienne	31, 43
Metaphorical Questions	48–49
Metaphors	17–21, 48–49
Minify	25, 26
Mund, Charles	3, 13, 67

N

Narrower Questions	47–48
Necessary Criteria	70
NGT-Storming	60, 63–64
Nominal Group Technique	60, 62–63
Nonverbal Behavior	94
Nonverbal Presentation	98–99

O

Object Rules	52–53
Opposite Questions	49
Osborne, Alex	25

P

Patience	99, 104–105
Petzing, James	16
Popcorn	88
Portman, John	22, 86
Precedence Questions	50
Presentation	95–99
Listening	99
Nonverbal	98–99
Timing	95
Verbal	97
Visual	98
Proverbs	36–38
Put to Other Uses	25, 26

Q

Question Breakdown	46–47, 62
Question Questing	60, 64–66
Questions	9, 11–12, 21–22, 45–55, 64
Broader	47–48
Consequence	50
Inside Out	49
List of	52–54
Metaphorical	48–49
Narrower	47–48
Opposite	49
Precedence	50
"Real"	50
Ridiculous	54–55

R

Rating Ideas	71–73
"Real" Questions	50
Rearrange	25, 26
Remindings	9, 10–11
Reverse	25, 26
Rewards	102–103
Ridiculous Questions	54–55
Rogers, Isaiah	86
Rouse, James	2, 91, 102
Rules	85–87
Rushmore, Stephen	103

S

Sack, Burton	34, 79, 82
SCAMPER	24–26, 62

Schank, Roger	10, 36, 37, 50, 51, 52–54
Schwabe, Linda	3, 103, 105, 107
Selection Criteria	70–71
Necessary	70
Desirable	71
Self Confidence	104
Selling Ideas	91–99
Sharpe, John L.	51
Simonson, Jim	10, 68, 79
Sledgehammers	76–89
Sloofman, H. Jay	41
Stern, Leslie W.	12, 14, 58, 85
Strand, Curt	3, 33
Strang, Donald	11, 102, 106
Substitute	25

T

Talbert, Keith	102
Tanuma, Chiaki	30, 102
Tatiboouet, Andre S.	1, 57, 68, 104
Tatibouet, Jane B.	42, 89, 101
Timing of Presentation	95
Tisch, Jonathan	30
Tremont House	86
Trice, Donald	2, 68, 81
Trust	95–96

V

Verbal Presentation	97
von Oech, Roger	79

W

Waters, Alice	42
Watson, Thomas J.	88
Weishaupt, Hans	34
Wilson, Trisha	84, 107
Winston, Carl H.	68, 88
Wright, Steven	83
Written Presentation	98

Y

Yesawich, Peter	13, 21, 51
Yonehama, Shoji	106
Young, John	21, 33